Trade in Counterfeit Goods and Free Trade Zones

EVIDENCE FROM RECENT TRENDS

This work is published under the responsibility of the Secretary-General of the OECD. The opinions expressed and arguments employed herein do not necessarily reflect the official views of the OECD member countries or the European Union Intellectual Property Office.

This document, as well as any data and any map included herein, are without prejudice to the status of or sovereignty over any territory, to the delimitation of international frontiers and boundaries and to the name of any territory, city or area.

Please cite this publication as:
OECD/EUIPO (2018), *Trade in Counterfeit Goods and Free Trade Zones: Evidence from Recent Trends*, OECD Publishing, Paris/EUIPO.
http://dx.doi.org/10.1787/9789264289550-en

ISBN 978-92-64-28954-3 (print)
ISBN 978-92-64-28955-0 (PDF)

The European Union
ISBN 978-92-9156-253-4 (print)
ISBN 978-92-9156-252-7 (PDF)

Catalogue number
TB-02-18-305-EN-C (print)
TB-02-18-306-EN-N (PDF)

The statistical data for Israel are supplied by and under the responsibility of the relevant Israeli authorities. The use of such data by the OECD is without prejudice to the status of the Golan Heights, East Jerusalem and Israeli settlements in the West Bank under the terms of international law.

Photo credits: Cover Illustration © Jeffrey Fisher.

Preface

Many countries have set up free trade zones (FTZs) to boost business activity and reap the benefits from free trade. These zones have been instrumental in the evolution of trade routes for the integrated supply chains of the global economy. However, FTZs may also facilitate illegal and criminal activities such as trade in counterfeit and pirated products, by providing a relatively safe environment, good infrastructure and light oversight.

To fully grasp the challenge of counterfeit and pirated trade and identify the best ways to address them, policy makers need evidence to document the links between FTZs and illicit trade, including trade in counterfeit and pirated goods. This is precisely the purpose of this study undertaken jointly by the OECD and the EUIPO, which sheds new light on the misuse of free trade zones for trade in counterfeit and pirated goods. We are also grateful to the World Customs Organization, the European Commission's Directorate-General for Taxation and Customs Union, and the United States Department of Homeland Security for providing the data, without which such a study could not have been conducted.

We are very pleased that our two institutions were able to co-operate to develop this solid and unique evidence based research. We are confident that the results of this work will facilitate the development of innovative policy options to respond to the challenges of trade in fake goods and other illicit commerce.

António Campinos
Executive Director, EUIPO

Marcos Bonturi
Director, OECD/GOV

Foreword

Many countries around the world have set up free trade zones (FTZs) as a way to spur economic development. FTZs provide tax advantages and other regulatory exemptions that have been a boost to trade facilitation, business formation and foreign investment. Research indicates that the number of FTZ is growing and that flows moving through them are expanding.

Even though FTZs bring clear economic benefits to their host economies, there is the possibility that they can be misused by criminal organisations to traffic and smuggle counterfeit and pirated goods. This raises the double concern of the impact of crime and illicit trade activities on good governance, public safety and the rule of law, as well as the negative effect that counterfeit trade has on legitimate competitive advantage of rights holders, and consequently on innovation, employment and long-term economic growth. The recent OECD-EU IPO report, *Mapping the Real Route of Trade in Fake Goods,* identified the risks posed by illicit trade in counterfeits transiting through FTZs, and the underlying challenges in terms of enforcement gaps. The findings led to the hypothesis that a significant portion of total illicit trade in fakes seem to transit through, or rely upon, FTZs, and that this needed further examination.

This joint OECD-EUIPO report investigates the empirical links between trade in counterfeit and pirated goods and free trade zones. The report provides robust empirical evidence that documents these links, building on previous studies carried out by the OECD and the EUIPO on trade in counterfeit and pirated goods. At the OECD, this study was supervised by the Task Force on Countering Illicit Trade (TF-CIT), which focuses on evidence-based research and advanced analytics to assist policy makers in mapping and understanding the market vulnerabilities exploited and created by illicit trade.

This report was prepared by Piotr Stryszowski, Senior Economist at the OECD Directorate for Public Governance jointly with Michał Kazimierczak, Economist at the European Observatory on Infringements of Intellectual Property Rights of the EUIPO, under the supervision of Stéphane Jacobzone, Deputy Head of Division, OECD and Nathan Wajsman, Chief Economist, EUIPO. The authors are grateful to Peter Avery and Florence Mouradian (OECD) and to Claire Castel (EUIPO) for their contributions.

The authors wish to thank the OECD experts, who provided valuable knowledge and insights: Rachel Bae, Dominique Guellec and Przemysław Kowalski. The authors would also like to thank experts from the OECD member countries and participants of several seminars and workshops for their valuable assistance provided. A special expression of appreciation is given to prof. Chirara Franzoni from Politecnico di Milano and to prof. Jean Marc Siroën from Université Paris Dauphine.

The quantitative research in this study relied on a global database on customs seizures, provided by the World Customs Organization (WCO) and supplemented with regional data submitted by the European Commission's Directorate-General for Taxation and Customs Union, the US Customs and Border Protection Agency and the US Immigration and Customs Enforcement. The authors express their gratitude for the data and for the valuable support of these institutions.

The OECD Secretariat wishes to thank Liv Gaunt, Kate Lancaster, Andrea Uhrhammer and Will Bromberg for their editorial and production support.

Table of contents

Tables

Figures

Boxes

Abbreviations

ASCM   Agreement on Subsidies and Countervailing Measures

BASCAP Business Action to Stop Counterfeiting and Piracy

CFZ   Colón Free Zone

CRS   Congressional Research Service

CSR   Corporate social responsibility

EUIPO   EU Intellectual Property Office

FATF   Financial Action Task Force

FDI   Foreign direct investment

FIAS   Foreign Investment Advisory Service

FTZ   Free trade zone

GATS   General Agreement on Trade in Services

GATT   General Agreement on Tariffs and Trade

GVC   Global value chains

ICC   International Chamber of Commerce

ILO   International Labour Organization

MFN   Most favoured nation

OECD   Organisation for Economic Co-operation and Development

TRIMS   Agreement on Trade-Related Investment Measures

UNCTAD United Nations Conference on Trade and Development

WCO   World Customs Organization

WTO   World Trade Organization

Executive Summary

Free trade zones (FTZs) have a long and cherished role in world trade, dating back to at least the early 1700s. They can provide numerous, unequivocal benefits to business and host countries. However, lightly regulated FTZs are also attractive to parties engaged in illegal and criminal activities, such as trade in counterfeit and pirated products or smuggling and money laundering, as these zones offer a relatively safe environment with both good infrastructure and limited oversight.

This study confirms the links between FTZs and trade in counterfeit products. The existence, number and size of FTZs in a country correlate with increases in the value of counterfeit and pirated products exported by that country's economy. An additional FTZ within an economy is associated with a 5.9% increase in the value of these problematic exports on average. The study also led to clear findings with respect to the connections between the value of fake goods exported from an economy on the one hand, and the number of firms operating in FTZs and the total value of exports from these zones on the other.

While FTZs were originally established as means to facilitate goods in transit by relieving traders of the need to complete many of the customs formalities that would otherwise apply to goods entering a country for consumption, these zones have evolved over time. They have developed into an important tool for attracting foreign investment and promoting economic development and growth, particularly in developing countries which can use them to leapfrog economic development. However, developed economies have also reaped the benefits of these zones, as evidenced by the several hundred zones operating in the United States alone.

Zones come in many forms, and they are subject to the specific laws and regulations of individual countries. The costs and benefits to businesses and host countries thus vary considerably from one economy to another. For businesses, zones provide numerous benefits, including savings in taxes and customs duties, greater flexibility in terms of labour and immigration rules than in the customs territory of host countries, lighter regulation and oversight of corporate activities, fewer restrictions on corporate activities, and additional opportunities to distribute goods to diverse markets. Furthermore, while there can be costs associated with choosing to locate in a zone, possibly including a range of special zone fees, this burden is often quite light, perhaps with even lower costs than would otherwise be incurred if the business were established in the customs territory of the host country.

For host countries, zones can be beneficial to economies to the extent that they attract foreign investment, create jobs and enhance export performance. The benefits to host countries, however, come at a cost, to the extent that governments are forced to forgo revenue, with any gains stemming from zone activities often failing to offset losses. Moreover, potential benefits to economies only apply to those zone activities that would otherwise not have been established in the customs territory of the given host country.

Beyond the economic costs and benefits to states and businesses, these lightly regulated zones are also attractive to parties engaged in illegal and criminal activities. Some zones may have indivertibly facilitated trade in counterfeit and pirated products, smuggling and money laundering. The problem is aggravated when governments do not police zones adequately. This can occur when zones are deemed to be foreign entities that are outside of the scope of domestic policing activities. When zones are operated by private entities, these entities' main interests are likely to be in finding ways to expand zone occupancy and provide profitable services to zone businesses. They may therefore have little direct interest in and/or capacity for conducting law enforcement activities. They may also lack the capacity or authority to effectively monitor zone operations. Even where government authorities are actively involved in overseeing zone activities, there is evidence that co-ordination between these authorities and zone operators, particularly private operators, can be weak, providing further scope for bad actors to exploit zones for their illicit activities.

More effective actions and co-ordination at the national and international levels are urgently needed to ensure that zones are not undermined by illicit activities. This has come to the attention of the OECD, EUIPO, European Anti-Fraud Office, Europol, the World Customs Organization, the World Trade Organization, Interpol, the United Nations Office on Drugs and Crime and the World Health Organization. The following organisations have made proposals to address the situation: the Caribbean Financial Action Task Force, the Black Market Peso Exchange System Multilateral Experts Working Group, the International Chamber of Commerce and the International Trademark Association. By working together the international community can ensure that FTZs continue to develop as important institutions that promote international trade without facilitating illicit activities. The two goals are not incompatible.

1. Evolution of Free Trade Zones

The 2017 OECD and EU Intellectual Property Office (EUIPO) report, *Mapping the Real Routes of Trade in Fake Goods* notes that parties that engage in the trade of counterfeit and pirated products tend to ship infringing products via complex routes, with many intermediate stops along the way (OECD/EUIPO, 2017[1]). The transit points are used to i) facilitate falsification of documents in ways that camouflage the original point of departure, ii) establish distribution centres for counterfeit and pirated goods, and iii) repackage or re-label goods. In addition, while imports of counterfeit goods are, in most cases, targeted by local enforcement authorities, goods in transit are often not within their scope, which means they are less likely to be intercepted.[1]

The transhipment operations are generally located in special economic zones that governments have created to stimulate economic activity. The zones, commonly referred to as free trade zones (FTZs), are designated areas that in most cases lie outside the customs jurisdiction of the economies concerned and are not subject to customs duties or most of the other customs procedures that would otherwise apply to imported merchandise (OECD/EUIPO, 2017[2]).[2] The 2017 report concludes that more in-depth analysis is needed in order to develop a clearer picture of the role that FTZs are now playing in facilitating trade in counterfeits.

The aim of this report is to provide further information and insights into FTZs, examining i) their evolution and the international legal framework in which they operate, ii) the reasons that countries have established zones and the benefits that zones provide to businesses, iii) the role they play in fuelling trade in counterfeit and pirated goods.

For hundreds of years, governments have sought ways to facilitate international trade in their ports. The earliest mechanisms were called free ports, which were designated areas open to commercial vessels on equal terms; cargoes destined for re-export were exempt from customs duties (Dictionary.com, 2017[3]). Such zones are still in operation. The first modern-day FTZ is generally considered to be the Shannon Free Zone, in Ireland. In the 1940s, Shannon Airport was an important refuelling station, with as much as 85% of transatlantic traffic stopping there to refuel (Shannon Chamber, 2017[4]). With the development of jet aircraft, however, the need for refuelling at Shannon declined significantly. The government responded by developing a programme that was designed to promote the area for industrial and tourism development; this included a number of tax and other benefits for firms that located there. The efforts succeeded; by 1965, exports of manufactured goods from Shannon accounted for almost one-third of the national total. The zone remains an important economic area, and it is currently home to more than 100 international and Irish companies that employ over 7 000 highly skilled employees and generate over EUR 3.3 billion in trade every year (Shannon Chamber, 2017[4]). The area remains one of the largest recipients of foreign investment in Ireland (Shannon Chamber, 2017[4]).

Zones have since experienced explosive growth worldwide, albeit in different forms. While generally referred to as free trade zones, the World Bank has coined the term "special economic zones" to capture the different forms they can take (FIAS, 2008[5]). These different types range from export processing zones, industrial areas focusing on assembly and manufacturing of intermediate imports aimed primarily, but not exclusively, at foreign markets, through free ports that typically encompass much larger areas and accommodate a broad range of activities, including tourism and retail sales to specially designated storage warehouses that are overseen by customs authorities.

The principal features of the different types of zones are that they:

- are geographically delimited, usually physically secured areas
- offer benefits based upon physical location within the zone
- represent separate, duty-free customs areas.

According to the International Labour Organization (ILO), the number of zones has increased from 79 zones located in 25 economies in 1975 to over 3 500 zones in 130 economies today. At last count, the zones collectively employed 66 million workers, while generating over USD 500 billion in direct trade-related value added (Table 1.1) (ILO, 2014[6]; Boyenge, 2007[7]).[3] Most of the zones in OECD countries were established prior to the 1970s, with a sharp rise occurring in other countries in the 1990s (FIAS, 2008). While the zones have proliferated in all regions worldwide, Asian zones account for some 85% of total zone workers worldwide, with China alone accounting for 40 million workers (ILO, 2014[6]). While there has been widespread growth, less than a dozen countries account for the majority of zone employment and exports (FIAS, 2008[5]).

Table 1.1. Trends in FTZ development. 1975-2006

	1975	1986	1997	2002	2006
Number of economies with zones	25	47	93	116	130
Number of zones	79	176	845	3000	3500
Employment (millions)	(1)	(1)	22.5	43	66

Note: [1] Not available
Source: (ILO, 2014[6])

Most enterprises in zones are engaged in labour-intensive assembly operations, notably in the apparel, textile and electric and electronics industries (Engman, Onodera and Pinali, 2007[8]; FIAS, 2008[5]; Farole and Akinci, 2011[9]; World Bank, 2017[10]). Female workers have traditionally accounted for 60-70% of the zone workforce worldwide, though the percentage has slipped as manufacturing activities in zones have expanded.

The development has varied by region.

- **Americas**: In the Americas, zones in many countries were developed by public sector entities, a situation which over time has given way to private zone development; in the process, a number of public zones were fully or partially privatised. The majority of the zones developed in recent years in South America, and particularly in Colombia and Uruguay, are "high-end" zones, offering state-of-the-art facilities and services.
- **Asia/Pacific**. The Asia/Pacific region has led zone development. Zones in East and South Asia are largely government run, either by central government authorities (e.g. Korea, Singapore and Bangladesh), by state government

corporations (Malaysia and India) or by ministerial departments (Chinese Taipei). Zone activities have focused largely on low-skilled textiles and apparel activities; a few, however, such as Thailand, Malaysia and Chinese Taipei, have expanded their activities into higher-skilled areas such as electronic and automotive assembly and chemical processing. Moreover, some countries have developed specialised zones for financial services, information technology and science-based industries.

- **Middle East and North Africa**: Although manufacturing is permitted in many zones in this area, trading and associated activities (such as packaging and repackaging) dominate. The Jebel Ali Free Zone in Dubai is a major regional distribution and logistics hub which serves as a model for other zones in the region.
- **Western Europe**: EU regulations restrict manufacturing and processing in zones, with few exceptions. The zones are largely located at ports and are publicly developed and managed.
- **Central and Eastern Europe and Central Asia**: In recent decades, many countries in this region have developed zones as a means of attracting foreign investment and integrating their economies into the global economy through expanded exports.
- **Sub-Saharan Africa**: Most zones in this region (with the exception of Ghana and Kenya) were developed and are run by governments. The dominant industries in the zones involve apparel/textiles and food processing.

The framework in which zones operate has changed markedly over time. Traditionally, zones were fairly isolated institutions, sealed off both in term of policy and in their geographic locations (FIAS, 2008[5]; Farole and Akinci, 2011[9]; World Bank, 2017[10]). Incentives and privileges were tightly controlled and qualifying firms typically had to be 80-100% export-oriented, engaged in recognised manufacturing activities and, at times, foreign-owned. Moreover, zone locations were found mainly in relatively remote areas or near transport hubs. Most were considered, like Shannon, to be instruments for the promotion of regional development. Moreover, they were developed and operated exclusively by governments.

This focus has undergone striking changes. Zone development is now largely viewed from a countrywide perspective. Indeed, each state in the United States have at least one FTZ (Bolle and Williams, 2013[11]). The role that zones can play in development has also changed (FIAS, 2008[5]). Zones in developing countries were previously viewed as a way to work around trade-restricted or closed economies. They were expected to increase exports, create jobs and transfer technology. Currently, zones are seen as broader mechanisms to promote two-way trade and facilitate liberalisation and modernisation in their host countries. An increased emphasis has been placed on encouraging linkages with domestic economies and promoting spill-over effects. As in the United States, the number of zones established in the inland areas of other countries has also increased.

Growth in the number of zones has been further spurred on by the expansion and liberalisation of the policies governing their use (FIAS, 2008[5]; Farole and Akinci, 2011[9]; World Bank, 2017[10]). These policy changes have included:

- an expansion of activities to include commercial and professional services
- equal treatment of foreign and domestic investors
- granting of incentives for private zone development
- relaxation or elimination of minimum export requirements.

Another notable change in zones over time has been the increasing role of privately run entities. In 1975, all zones were government-owned and government-operated (FIAS, 2008[5]; Farole and Akinci, 2011[9]; World Bank, 2017[10]). By the mid-2000s, some 62% of zones in developing and transition economies had been developed and were being operated by private entities (Table 1.2). The proliferation of private actors in zone development and management stems, in part, from the tendency for private zones to be more efficient. It is also due to the potential cost savings for governments. When zones are privately developed, less government funding is often needed, as private developers finance onsite infrastructure and facilities, with governments focusing on building offsite infrastructure and facilities which may represent only 25% of onsite costs. Moreover, most private zone operators are required to take on the expense of constructing onsite facilities for the use of the government authorities involved with zone operations. They may also assume certain regulatory functions on behalf of customs agencies, thereby reducing customs costs for governments.

Table 1.2. Private and public sector zones, by region, circa 2007[1]

Region	Public	Private	Percent private
Americas	146	394	73
Asia/Pacific	435	556	56
Sub-Saharan Africa	49	65	57
Middle East and North Africa	173	40	19
Central and Eastern Europe and Central Asia	69	374	84
Total	**872**	**1,429**	**62**

Note: [1] Excludes single factory programmes.
Source: (FIAS, 2008[5]).

The FIAS (2008)[5] assessment concludes that the growth in private involvement has been beneficial, as privately-run zones tend to offer better facilities and amenities, command higher prices from tenants and attract higher-end tenants. Many public sector zones, in contrast, have crowded, poorly designed and inadequately maintained facilities, reflecting the budgetary and operational constraints that they face. Moreover, privately-run zones tend to be more responsive to tenant needs, providing a wider range of property management services and amenities (Box 1.1). Many private zones also appear to achieve better economic outcomes with respect to exports, employment, foreign direct investment, and social and environmental impact.

Box 1.1. Free trade zone facilities and services

Free trade zone facilities and services have expanded over time, due to the interest on the part of private zone operators in providing tenants with attractive options, including:

- childcare facilities
- medical clinics
- conference centres
- product exhibition areas
- commercial centres
- training facilities
- shelter plans
- repair and maintenance centres
- shared bonded warehouse facilities
- incubator facilities
- on-site banking facilities
- on-site housing
- on-site customs clearance and trade logistics facilities
- high-speed telecommunications and Internet services, networked buildings

Source : (FIAS, 2008[5]).

Notes

[1] The analysis in this report refers to goods that are placed in free trade zones, and does not refer to "goods in transit", as referred to Article 5 of GATT.

[2] It should be noted some hosting economies do have customs controls in the FTZ.

[3] UNCTAD (2015) indicates that the number of zones now exceeds 4 000.

References

Dictionary.com (2017), *Definition of free port*, http://www.dictionary.com/browse/free-port (accessed on 9 December 2017). [3]

FIAS (2008), *Special economic zone: performance lessons learned, and implication for zone development*, Foreign Investment Advisory Service (FIAS) occasional paper, World Bank, Washington, D.C. [5]

OECD/EUIPO (2017), *Mapping the Real Routes of Trade in Fake Goods*, OECD Publishing, http://dx.doi.org/10.1787/9789264278349-en.. [1]

OECD/EUIPO (2017), *Mapping the Real Routes of Trade in Fake Goods*, OECD Publishing, Paris, http://dx.doi.org/10.1787/9789264278349-en. [2]

Shannon Chamber (2017), *Shannon Chamber website*, http://www.shannonchamber.ie. [4]

2. Benefits and costs of zones for host economies and business

Zones provide numerous benefits to business. The advantages can include savings in taxes and customs duties, more flexible labour rules than those applicable in the customs territories of host countries, laxer regulation and oversight of corporate activities, fewer restrictions on corporate activities and opportunities to improve distribution of goods to diverse markets. Meanwhile, the costs for choosing to locate in a zone, which might include a variety of special zone fees, are often quite low, perhaps even lower than would otherwise be the case if the business were established in the customs territory of the host country.

In both developing and developed host economies, zones can function, and in practice have been used, to promote economic development. The potential benefits are greatest for the latter group of economies, where the zones are often instrumental in attracting foreign investment (particularly in high-tech industries), creating jobs (particularly higher-skill positions) and enhancing export performance. The benefits for host countries, however, come at a cost, to the extent that governments are reduced and not compensated by any revenue stemming from zone activities often failing to offset losses. Moreover, potential benefits to economies apply only to those zone activities which would not otherwise have been established in the customs territory of the host country. It is not easy to single out occasions when zone status may have played a decisive role in ensuring that a business was set up or maintained in a given country. Of course, after an investment decision has already been made, businesses can then seek out zone status if they believe that it will help them enhance their performance.

Beyond the revenue implications for governments, lightly regulated zones are also attractive to parties engaged in illegal and criminal activities. Zones have facilitated trade in counterfeit and pirated products, as well as smuggling and money laundering, and they have often provided bad actors with a relatively safe environment in which to carry out their illicit activities. The problem is aggravated in instances where governments do not control zones adequately; this can occur when zones are deemed to be foreign entities that are outside of the scope of domestic policing activities. It can be further compounded when zones are operated by private entities. These parties' main interests are likely to be in finding ways to expand zone occupancy and provide profitable services to zone businesses. They may therefore have little direct interest in and/or capacity for conducting law enforcement activities, and they may lack the capacity or authority to effectively monitor zone operations. Even where government authorities are actively involved in overseeing zone activities, there is evidence that co-ordination between these authorities and zone operators, particularly those that are private parties, can be weak, thus opening up space for bad actors to exploit zones for their illicit activities.

Implications for host economies

The rationale for government support for zones has changed over time. As discussed above, the initial purpose of zones was to facilitate the movement of goods being transhipped through intermediary ports by waiving normal customs procedures. The success that the Shannon zone had in spurring regional development in a depressed economic zone and the subsequent similar sorts of success in China brought about a change in thinking, as governments saw zones as a mechanism that could be employed in support of their broader economic aims.

The change in the focus of zones is reflected in the case of the United States. Legislation providing for the establishment of foreign-trade zones was passed in 1934, with a view towards expediting and encouraging foreign commerce in light of the effects of the increase in tariffs under the Smoot-Hawley Tariff Act of 1930 (Foreign-Trade Zones Resource Center, 2017[12]; Wikipedia Contributors, 2017[13]) was expected at that time that zones would be used primarily for warehousing and transhipment or for minor processing and subsequent exportation of products, which would help to reduce the administrative burdens associated with bonded warehouses and the processing of duty drawback claims (USITC, 1984[14]).

The US programme had its limitations, however, as reflected by the fact that in the years 1936-65 less than 10 zones were authorised. In 1950, manufacturing operations became authorised, but interest in zones only grew significantly in the early 1980s, when the Treasury Department issued administrative rulings indicating that manufacturers did not have to pay duties on value added in zones when goods were imported into US customs territory, nor on brokerage and transportation fees (Bolle and Williams, 2013[11]). By 2015, there were 186 active zones, with a total of 324 active production (Foreign-Trade Zones Board, 2016[15]). Employment topped 420 000, and shipments of foreign and domestic merchandise into the zones totalled nearly USD 660 billion, while exports to foreign countries amounted to over USD 85 billion.

While business has boomed in these zones, questions have been raised about the effects on the US economy as a whole, prompting a number of government reports since the early 1980s. A 1984 report by the US International Trade Commission (USITC, 1984[14]) came to the following conclusions:

- Zones had accounted for a growing volume of trade and had served effectively as transhipment points.
- Direct and indirect employment had grown substantially, but the jobs created were not necessarily "new". A similar conclusion was reached in an assessment carried out by the General Accounting Office, in 1984 (GAO, 1984[16]).
- The domestic content of merchandise exported abroad from zones had not been very considerable.
- It was not clear whether or not the economic activity in zones would otherwise have taken place in the absence of the zones. Moreover, in the case of manufacturing/assembly operations, it was noted that the benefits conferred to zone firms could in some cases result in the loss of tariff protection to domestic suppliers and affect competition in finished products, to the benefit of companies operating in zones.

The report presents the views and recommendations of labour and US firms, as well as those of zone users. The former groups raised concerns about issues such as duty reductions and decreased customs presence and control. They contended that zones had resulted in a net decrease in US employment and had stimulated imports rather than boosting exports, thereby damaging domestic industries and suppliers and their employees. A 1988 update to the 1984 USITC report concluded in fact that the US auto parts industry had been adversely affected by zone activities, while the auto assembly industry had benefitted (USITC, 1988[17]). Zone users and proponents, on the other hand, contended that zones had a dynamic ripple effect on the local and national economy, attracting foreign investment while exerting a positive effect on the US balance of payments (USITC, 1984[14]).

Another analysis carried out by the General Accounting Office in 1989 focused on the need to address issues related to the administration and operation of zones, while yet another report by the Congressional Research Service (CRS) in 2013 highlighted security issues and provided an overall assessment of the zone programme (GAO, 1989[18]; Bolle and Williams, 2013[11]). The CRS report concludes that FTZs could potentially benefit the economy as a whole, to the extent that the savings accorded manufacturers from tariff reductions, administrative efficiencies, tax benefits and duty deferral encouraged US corporations to maintain operations in the US and provided an incentive for foreign producers to invest in manufacturing plants in the country. This in turn would potentially help communities hold on to businesses and the jobs associated with them. Consumers were likely to benefit from the cost savings, while federal, state and local tax revenues could also grow thanks to increased economic activity resulting both directly and indirectly from the zones.

On the other hand, zone activities were seen as possibly exacting costs on the US economy, particularly i) for domestic producers of the components being imported into zones, particularly to the extent that they lost tariff protection, and, eventually, ii) for domestic producers of the items produced in zones (Bolle and Williams, 2013[11]). Moreover, the tariff reductions could result in a loss of US tax revenue. It was also noted that zone critics had argued that the benefits of zones brought with them distorted competition, favouring a small number of businesses.

Numerous studies and assessments have also been carried out with respect to the situation in developing countries, where the focus has been on the role that zones could play in boosting export competitiveness and overall economic development. In this regard, Papadopoulus and Malhotra (2007)[20] developed a useful framework for assessing the broader potential economic benefits that zones could provide for countries, distinguishing the direct effects from the longer-term externalities, which eventually could be far more valuable, in particular to developing countries (Table 2.1).

Table 2.1. Typology of potential benefits of zones to host countries

Area	Potential benefits
Direct benefits:	
1. Exports	Increased exports increase foreign exchange reserves and improve the balance of payments.
2. Local supply chains	More business for domestic producers who sell inputs needed by zone-based firms.
3. FDI	Increased currency inputs, enhances the host country's capital formation process.
4. Employment	More jobs (that might have gone elsewhere).
5. Incomes	Wages may be lower than in developed countries but can be higher than in the host's domestic territory and can rise rapidly over time.
Long-term externalities:	
1. Technology and knowledge transfer	This is distinct from FDI, which does not necessarily entail such transfers.
2. Labour skills	The employability of workers outside the zones is enhanced and has implication throughout the economy.
3. Regional development	Zones can be established selectively in areas that can best capitalize on an economy's strengths and/or that need new business activity the most.
4. Infrastructure	Development of an efficient industrial infrastructure is critical for a successful zone program; it enables the host country to compete more effectively for FDI.
5. Support services	Successful zone require banking, legal, consulting, telecom, and other similar support services that, once developed for the zone(s), benefit the nation as a whole.
6. Controlled/partial deregulation	Enables host to participate in the international economy without compromising national policies or political ideologies.
7. Deregulation models	Where deregulation is desired, zones enable the testing of models prior to applying them nationally.
8. Broader catalyst and demonstration effects	Overall economic modernization, especially because EPZs help to attract foreign firms that might not otherwise have invested in the country

Source: Adapted from Papadopoulus and Malhotra (2007)[20].

The potential benefits are, however, sometimes questioned by critics who cast doubt on the value of the activities that zones attract and their poor records on labour rights and working conditions (Table 2.2). Adverse effects cited by labour organisations include human rights violations in the workplace, corruption among government zone managers, support for the informal or underground economy, low levels of tech transfer, labour migration to urban zones that cannot handle the influxes and an overdependence on zone investors who may tend to withdraw their investments when wages in zones rise (Papadopoulus and Malhotra, 2007[19]).

Table 2.2. Views of zone critics

Area	Zone critics
Foreign exchange earnings	Zones host import-dependent activities with low value-added.
Industrial activity	Zones perpetuate low-skilled assembly operations.
Policy reform	Zones help avoid countrywide reforms.
FDI	Zones attract FDI in low-tech, low-skilled activities.
Women	Zones segregate women and pay them lower wages.
Labour rights	Zones suppress labour rights.
Working conditions	Zones allow companies to get away with poor workplace health and safety conditions.
Environment	Zones exercise lax environmental controls in order to attract polluting industries.

Source: (FIAS, 2008[5]).

FIAS (2008)[5] reviews the situation in key areas, concluding that:

- Zones have proven to be highly effective at generating employment, especially for women, particularly in smaller countries. While there are exceptions (particularly with government-run zones), wage and working conditions tend to be better in zones than in the rest of the host economy.
- Zones can be effective at increasing the volume and diversity of exports.
- Zones can be an important tool for attracting foreign direct investment, offsetting what might be an adverse investment climate in a country.
- Commercial linkages with the local economy can be strengthened as shipments to zones are typically considered exports and therefore eligible for export benefits.
- Although this is not always the case, zones can sometimes serve as proving grounds where new policies can be implemented and tested on an experimental basis, prior to more widespread adoption in countries.

These conclusions are supported by other assessments at the individual country level. A review of studies on six government managed zones in Asia that was carried out in 2003 concluded that the zones, located in Korea, Malaysia, Sri Lanka, China and Indonesia, were unambiguously economically efficient and generated returns well above the estimated opportunity costs in those countries (Table 2.3) (Jayanthakumaran, 2003[20]). The zones were an important source of jobs in all cases, and they were found to support local entrepreneurs in the cases of Korea and Indonesia. The result for the Philippines, on the other hand, resulted in a net negative present value, reflecting the country's high infrastructure expenditures in setting up the profiled zone.

Table 2.3. Realisation of expected benefits of selected zones in Korea, Philippines, Indonesia, Malaysia, Sri Lanka and China

Expected benefit	Korea	Philippines	Indonesia	Malaysia	Sri Lanka	China
Employment	✓	✓	✓	✓	✓	✓
Foreign exchange earnings	✓	✓	x	✓	-	✓
Domestic raw materials	✓	x	✓	✓	✓	-
Domestic capital equipment	x	x	x	✓	x	-
Taxes and other revenues	✓	✓	✓	✓	✓	✓
Domestic profit	-	-	-	-	✓	x
Electricity use	x	x	x	x	x	x
Domestic borrowing	x	x	x	x	x	-

Notes: "✓" = realised; "x"=not realised
Source: (Jayanthakumaran, 2003[20]).

Other examples of success stories include Shenzhen in China and Mauritius (Papadopoulus and Malhotra, 2007[19]). Shenzhen grew from a small town of 20 000 in 1979, to city of 3.5 million with a high GDP per capita, and with many multinational firms operating in the area. Mauritius set up a zone in 1971, helping it to become one of Africa's leading exporters of merchandise, while reducing its reliance on sugar exports. In the process, export earnings rose by annual rate of 80% in the 1980s, and unemployment fell from 20% in 1971 to less than 2% in 1994, resulting in a need to import labour.

In transition economies and other developing countries, the zones studied tended to experience difficulties early on, but their performance improved over time as reforms were made, one of the more notable of which involved opening up the development and management of zones to private parties (FIAS, 2008[5]). The programmes in Europe and Central Asia were seen, on the whole, to have experienced moderate success, led by those in Poland, Bulgaria and Romania. Programmes in the CIS, on the other hand, were seen as having had to face barriers that limited their beneficial effects.

Further evidence of the benefits and costs of zones is provided by FIAS (2008)[5], which details implication for i) employment, ii) exports, iii) foreign direct investment, iv) industrial upgrading and technology transfer; v) foreign exchange earnings, vi) budgetary impacts, vii) social and environmental impacts (including labour standards, pay and working conditions, human resource development, and environmental impacts) and viii) impact on country-wide reforms. Following is an overview of the situation in terms of these key elements, based on the FIAS (2008)[5]'s assessment.

2.1. Employment

Zones play an important role in some economies thanks to the jobs they provide (FIAS, 2008[5]). Globally, the percentage of employment accounted for by zones is 0.21%. In Honduras, zones account for 4.6% of employment, and the levels are even higher in the Dominican Republic (6.2%), Tunisia (8%), Fiji (10%), the Seychelles (12%), Mauritius (24%) and the UAE (25%).

2.2. Exports

Some reports suggest that the volume of world trade channelled through zones is as much as 20%, and that the share in developing economies is much higher, about 40% overall (Table 2.4) (Papadopoulus and Malhotra, 2007[19]; FIAS, 2008[5]). Moreover, the share of many countries' exports passing through zones exceeded 70% (With respect to diversification, zones have proven to be effective mechanisms for expanding exports of manufactured goods . Most Caribbean and Central American economies, for example, exported mainly fruit and vegetables prior to the establishment of zones. In Costa Rica, the share of manufactured exports rose from less than 10% in 1990 to 55% in 2003. Over the same period, the main exports from zones there evolved from apparel and textile products to electronic components, which by 2003 accounted for over half of zone exports. Many other countries had similar experiences.

Table 2.5).

Table 2.4. Exports from developing countries from zones, by area

Area	Total value (millions of USD)	Percentage of total exports
Asia/Pacific	510 666	41
Americas	72 636	39
Central and Eastern Europe and Central Asia	89 666	39
Middle East and North Africa	169 459	36
Sub-Saharan Africa	8 605	49
Total of above	851 032	41

Source: (FIAS, 2008[5]).

With respect to diversification, zones have proven to be effective mechanisms for expanding exports of manufactured goods (FIAS, 2008[5]). Most Caribbean and Central American economies, for example, exported mainly fruit and vegetables prior to the establishment of zones. In Costa Rica, the share of manufactured exports rose from less than 10% in 1990 to 55% in 2003. Over the same period, the main exports from zones there evolved from apparel and textile products to electronic components, which by 2003 accounted for over half of zone exports. Many other countries had similar experiences.

Table 2.5. Share of zone exports in total exports of selected economies, 2005

Region	Economy	Zone export share (%)
Americas	Nicaragua	79
	Dominican Republic	77
	Panama	67
Asia/Pacific	Bangladesh	76
	Sri Lanka	67
	Philippines	78
	Pakistan	50
Sub-Saharan Africa	Ghana	22
	Madagascar	80
	Mauritius	34

Source: (FIAS, 2008[5])

2.2.1. *Foreign direct investment*

Zones can be an important destination for foreign direct investment (FDI) in some countries. A 2002 UNCTAD analysis concluded that the relationship between the location of foreign affiliates and the location of zones seems weak (UNCTAD, 2002[21]). That said, in some countries the share of FDI accounted for by zones was quite high: in the Philippines, zones accounted for 81% of FDI in 2000; in Bangladesh, two zones accounted for 32% of FDI; in Mexico, zones received 31% of the total manufacturing FDI between 1994 and 2001. Moreover, in Costa Rica some 75% of all foreign affiliates were located in zones, suggesting a significant FDI link. In China, zones accounted for over 80% of cumulative FDI at the start of the millennium (FIAS, 2008[5]).

2.2.2. *Industrial upgrading and technology transfer*

Some assessments have indicated that the skill levels of workers in zones have remained relatively static, citing cases in which little change has occurred over time (FIAS, 2008). A case study of Mexico carried out in 2002 concluded that zones in that country had been very successful at creating jobs and alleviating unemployment (Blanco de Armas and Sadni-Jallap, 2002[22]). The skill levels of zone workers, however, were notably lower than those outside the zone, with little growth experienced between 1988 and 1998. Although there was evidence of some modernisation and upgrading of skills in the zones, it was not clear that this had spread to other parts of the economy. Due to the high import component of zone operations and the low skill level of the work force, the activities of the zones were not expected to contribute to significant industrial upgrading in the country at large.

Assessments in other countries, however, have shown a more positive relationship between zones and industrial upgrading, in particular in economies in East Asia; Korea, Chinese Taipei, Malaysia and the Philippines were notable in this regard (FIAS, 2008[5]). A recent assessment of zones in Panama also finds a positive relationship (Haussman, Obach and Santos, 2016[23]). FIAS (2008)[5] concludes, however, that most research indicates that there are no significant differences between zone and non-zone-based export-oriented firms in terms of technology transfer and linkages.

2.2.3. Foreign exchange earnings

The success of zones in generating foreign exchange earnings from exports depends on the value-added in zones, which in turn is influenced by the extent to which local inputs are used in zones. Zones that have been particularly successful in this regard include Korea, which was successful in developing backward supply linkages and sub-contracting relationships with domestic firms, particularly in footwear operations. Value-added was over 60% in 2000, with figures of 62% for Indonesia in 1990, and 45% for the Philippines in 2003 (FIAS, 2008[5]). Other zones which demonstrated growth in value-added activities include Mauritius (where value-added rose from 23% in 1980 to 41% in 1995), Costa Rica (an increase from 18% in 1996 to 40% in 2000), Honduras (from 3.3% in 1990 to 24.5% in 1995, and El Salvador (from 3.8% in 1990 to 20.4 % in 1996).

Some other zones did not fare as well, notably those in Mexico, where the export ratio held at 30% from 1991 to 2000, and the Dominican Republic, where the ratio fell from 40-45% in the early 1980s to 25-30% by the end of the decade (FIAS, 2008[5]). Elsewhere, the export ratios of countries such as Nicaragua, Guatemala and Sri Lanka were all less than 10% in the 1990s. A number of factors have contributed to the failure to develop linkages, including:

- high import ratios of most zone activities: apparel, footwear and electronics operations have import ratios of 60-85%
- the impact of export access agreements that, for example, provide incentives for zone operators to import materials from the county that they will eventually export to
- bans on local sales by firms in zones, which might contribute to discouraging forward linkages
- a lack of competitiveness of local firms
- preferences on the part of global firms for international suppliers
- a lack of awareness and information about potential domestic suppliers.

2.2.4. Budgetary impact

The budgetary impact of zones on governments depends on the scope and magnitude of incentives provided to zone users (Box 2.1). Firstly, reduced corporate income tax provisions, import duty exemptions and indirect tax abatements all contribute to reducing government revenues, without necessarily providing a benefit to the country concerned; a benefit is only realised if the investments in a zone operation would not have occurred in the absence of the incentives offered (FIAS, 2008[5]).

Box 2.1. Government costs and revenues form zone operations

Potential revenues

- corporate income taxes
- personal income taxes
- permit fees and service charges
- rental or sales fees
- import duties on products sold locally
- concession fees for utilities and the like that are linked to the zones

Potential costs

- wages for staff to oversee and/or manage zone operations
- internal and/or external infrastructure
- import duties lost due to smuggling
- tax revenue lost when firms relocate from the domestic customs territory to zones
- subsidies

Source : FIAS, 2008.

On the other hand, governments tend to reap gains from the personal income taxes paid by zone employees and income from tariffs assessed on merchandise imported into the host country (FIAS, 2008[5]). These revenues can be substantial. In the case of Madagascar, over 20% of employers' social contributions are sourced from zone companies, and the companies contributed 2% of the country's GDP in 1998. In the case of government-run zones, revenue is also raised from fees and service charges and land and building rentals and sales.

Zones can become financial drains if they require large outlays for onsite and/or offsite infrastructure, if the zones are not operated on a cost-recovery basis, and/or if they receive subsidised inputs, such as utilities and services (FIAS, 2008[5]). Earlier zones established in developing countries often incurred costs that were absorbed by host jurisdictions. More attention, however, has been paid in recent periods to reducing such costs, particularly with respect to infrastructure outlays.

2.2.5. Social and environmental impact

A 2015 UNCTAD analysis looked at the performance of zones in advancing general environmental and social goals linked to sustainable development (UNCTAD, 2015[24]). The report examines the situation in 100 zones in 20 emerging economies. It concludes that most zones do not have in place mechanisms to support good environmental and social practices. The weakest area was in corporate governance; very few zones provided assistance for companies to combat corruption.

Labour standards, pay and working conditions

Concerns have been raised in the past about zone issues related to gender, wage levels and benefits, workers' rights, working conditions and environmental impact (FIAS, 2008[5]). The situation has improved over time, with significant progress made in changing the anti-union and labour suppressing aspects of some zones. In 2003, the ILO and International Confederation of Free Trade Unions, however, raised the following concerns about zone operations in a number of countries (FIAS, 2008[5]):

- restrictions on freedom of association and collective bargaining
- failure to recognise the right to strike
- non-observance of national labour legislation.

There are also concerns about weak labour inspection practices, intimidation of workers, limited access to zones by labour organisers, formation of company-controlled unions and other anti-union practices (FIAS, 2008[5]). In addition, women's rights have been raised as an issue in some zones, notably with respect to equal pay and to policies concerning pregnancy and child care.

An assessment of the situation suggests that problems are not pervasive, affecting only a fraction of zones worldwide (FIAS, 2008[5]). Wages can be higher in zones than outside them, and foreign multinationals located in zones maintain occupational health and safety practices which are often better than those maintained by domestic enterprises outside zones. Moreover, adverse labour and social policies are most closely associated with zones developed and run by governments.

Human resource development

While there have been claims that zones fall short in promoting an upgrading of skills in their host economies, there is evidence that in some places spill-overs have been significant, especially in zones catering to higher value-added industries or more knowledge-intensive zones (FIAS, 2008[5]). Zones in Malaysia, the Dominican Republic, Thailand, the Philippines and Mauritius stand out specifically in this regard.

Environmental impact

Environmental performance has raised questions in a number of jurisdictions, including Mexico and older zones in Sri Lanka, the Dominican Republic and Mauritius (FIAS, 2008[5]). Recently constructed zones and those not scattered throughout a country tend to exhibit better performance; in these instances, effective environmental management is a key selling point to potential zone tenants.

2.2.6. Special economic zones and countrywide reforms

Zones have often been viewed as a mechanism for addressing the anti-export bias of countries, thereby offering a second-best solution (the preferred solution being countrywide reform) (FIAS, 2008[5]). In this context, zones could serve as a means to temporarily address these biases until broader reforms are introduced. Having such a temporary solution in place could, however, actually slow the impetus for reforms. On a national level, the debate focuses on whether zones serve as catalysts for reforms, or whether on the contrary they actually slow reforms. Analysis suggests that zones in Korea, Jordan and Kuwait served as catalysts, while those in the Dominican Republic and Tunisia did not. In Korea, the zone programme launched in 1970 promoted economy-wide structural reforms, with expanding linkages between zones and the local economy. In contrast, little integration occurred in the Dominican Republic in the 30 years following the establishment of the first zone.

China, Malaysia, Jamaica, Kuwait and Jordan have used zones to test the impact of potential new policies that would then be applied countrywide (FIAS, 2008[5]). Market-oriented reforms to FDI regulations and land and tax policies were first introduced and tested in zones in China, before being implemented countrywide. In Jamaica, telecommunications deregulation was first tried in zones, before being introduced more generally. In Panama and India, more flexible labour policies were being tried out in zones, as a precursor to broader reforms. In the Middle East, zones were used to test the effects of liberalisation of FDI.

2.2.7. Global value chains

In its assessment, FIAS (2008)[5] argues that zones can continue to play an important role in developing and developed countries alike, provided they evolve in response to global integration and regional free trade agreements. The United Nations Conference on Trade and Development (UNCTAD) explored the possible way forward in its work on global value chains (UNCTAD, 2013[25]).

The UNCTAD assessment notes that multinational corporations are increasingly under pressure to demonstrate corporate social responsibility (CSR) in their operations worldwide. Indeed, codes of conduct have been developed by a number of organisations to this end, the OECD Guidelines for Multinational Enterprises being a prime example. The ability of firms to exercise CSR has become more fraught in light of the development of global value chains (GVCs), as firms may face difficulties in influencing the behaviour of their affiliates and suppliers worldwide.

It has been noted that zones are already important hubs for GVC activities, and that they are in good position to be used by governments and businesses to further CSR objectives. This is especially the case when zones can be transformed into centres of excellence that meet high standards, which can be an effective mechanism to promote CSR-acceptable behaviour and practices among affiliates and suppliers worldwide (UNCTAD, 2013). Creating such an environment is seen as enhancing the ability of zones to attract and retain FDI.

There are, however, challenges to be met if zones are to be transformed. A survey carried out by UNCTAD of 100 zones in 20 emerging countries in 2013 concluded that only a handful of pioneering zones provided an environment that was highly supportive of CSR/sustainability objectives. The initiatives of the leading zones included: i) support for the formulation and implementation of responsible labour practices, ii) well-developed environmental reporting requirements, iii) policies and regulations governing occupational health and safety, iv) mechanisms to assist firms in combating corruption. With respect to the latter requirement (combatting corruption), few zones had addressed the matter, and the response seems to have been weak in those that did (UNCTAD, 2015[24]).

2.3. For business

The benefits offered to businesses locating in zones has expanded over time, moving from simple import duty exemptions to include advantageous corporate tax rates, exemptions from indirect and local taxes, unrestricted repatriation of capital and profits and unrestricted management of foreign exchange (FIAS, 2008[5]). Moreover, zones in the Middle East and North Africa often go further, providing personal income tax exemptions for expatriate workers and zero corporate income taxation, in perpetuity. Zones in the United Arab Emirates, for example, are able to bring in foreign labour at pay rates that are below those mandated for workers outside the zone, and with fewer benefits.

As discussed in the section on global value chains, zones can play an important role for firms engaged in international commerce, providing them with opportunities to create exchange networks and achieve nearly seamless supply and marketing chains as part of an international system, while operating under highly advantageous trade and FDI regimes (Papadopoulus and Malhotra, 2007[19]). Coupled with import-oriented zones, zones can be viewed as important parts of a "virtual network" that can enable the production, movement and marketing of goods in a barrier-free environment from their conception to just before the final sale.

Table 2.6 sets out some of the key potential benefits that firms can capture by operating in zones. The first part of the table identifies those benefits that are available in developed and developing countries alike, while the second part lists the general benefits that can be attained by operating in developing countries. The table is followed by a brief description of these and other benefits.

Table 2.6. Potential benefits for international firms locating in zones

Benefits specific to zones
1. Duty-free imports
2. Avoidance of duties/taxes on waste or consumed materials
3. Simplified administrative procedures
4. Lower insurance costs (premiums based on duty-free value of items)
5. Lower inventory costs through centralised warehousing
6. Flexibility in bulk-breaking, packaging and labelling for different foreign markets, while benefitting from duty-free status
7. In light of the above, more cost-effective position as a central distribution hub
8. Product assembly or manufacture in a duty-free environment
9. Tax and other concessions beyond duty savings
10. Duty-free import of capital equipment
11. Lighter environmental and labour regulations
12. Right to establish fully-owned or majority-controlled enterprises
13. Full repatriation of profits and/or capital
14. Superior and often subsidised infrastructure
15. Greater protection against crime as zone perimeters are normally secured by host countries
16. Dynamic zone improvement environment as zone operators seek to maintain and enhance their competitiveness in relation to other zones

Benefits associated with location in a developing country generally
1. Inexpensive labour
2. Plentiful labour
3. Access to raw and intermediate materials
4. Access to large internal markets
5. Strategic country locations near major target markets for exports

Source: Adapted from Papadopoulus and Malhotra (2007)[20].

2.3.1. Inventory control

Zones can be advantageous when used to stock goods so as to avoid peak season freight rates, with companies thereby achieving reductions in landed costs (Hainsworth, 2017[26]). The stocking of goods in zones also allows businesses to manage inventory in a cost-effective manner, avoiding what in some instances can be significant import duties if the goods in question are destined for the local market (Hainsworth, 2017[27]).

2.3.2. Fiscal incentives

Duty-deferral and duty-free treatment of exports are basic features of all zones. Exemptions from or reductions in inventory taxes, excise taxes and local taxes also exist in some places. Other incentives vary considerably from zone to zone. One of the more generous programmes in this regard is found in the United Arab Emirates. As shown in Box 2.2, corporate income and personal income are exempt from taxes.

Box 2.2. Profile of Jafza Free Trade Zone

The Jafza Free Trade Zone in Dubai was created in 1985. It is currently operated by DP World, which is a company specialising in marine terminal management. The zone has grown from a small operation of 19 companies into a business community of over 7 000 companies from more than 100 countries, employing over 144 000 workers. It accounts for more than 32% of foreign direct investment in the United Arab Emirates, and more than 50% of Dubai's exports. For investors, location in the zone offers:

- 100% foreign ownership
- 0% corporate tax for 50 years (a concession that is renewable)
- no restrictions on capital repatriation
- 0% import or re-export duties
- 0% personal income tax
- no currency restrictions
- no restriction on foreign talent or employees
- ability to mortgage premises to a bank or financing company
- onsite customs.

In order to form a company within the zone, investors are required to choose between i) a Free Zone Establishment, which is essentially a limited liability company (LLC), with one shareholder, ii) a Free Zone Company, which is an LLC with up to 50 shareholders, iii) a Public Listed Company, which is an LLC that can offer shares to the public or iv) a Branch of a Company, which is 100% owned by its corporate parent (which is located outside the zone) and bears its name. Operating licences are required, with their nature depending on the type of activities to be carried out.

Sources: (Jafza, 2017[28]; DP World, 2018[29])

Zones can also sometimes be used to reduce duties on products that are processed or manufactured there and then shipped into the host country's market. This occurs in cases when the tariff structure is "inverted" (i.e. when the tariff rates on a finished product are lower than those applicable to the inputs used to make that product). In the case of the United States, for example, tariffs on many finished pharmaceutical products are "zero" while the tariffs on the active ingredients used to make those products are significant (British American Business, 2017[30]).

Moreover, as mentioned in Table 2.2, duties on waste or materials consumed in the manufacturing of a finished product can be avoided when the product is imported into the host country; also, the domestic value-added to goods manufactured in zones is not taxable. Finally, as no duties on exports are applied, the duty draw-back procedures that would otherwise apply to goods re-exported from a host country can be avoided.

2.3.3. Simplified customs procedures

Customs procedures for zones may differ significantly from those applicable to goods entering a country directly. In the United States, for example, reporting for goods entering zones is subject to a "Weekly Entry" provision which allows importers to report to customs once per week instead of once per shipment. This can result in direct savings, as the merchandise processing fee assessed for each formal entry processed by customs would only be applied once, at a maximum cost of USD 485 (Foreign-Trade Zones Resource Center, 2017[12]; U.S. Customs and Border Protection, 2017[31]).

2.3.4. Zone-to-zone transfers

Goods can often move between zones without duties being assessed (Ferguson and Steverango, 2013[32]). Goods associated with low-risk/repetitive shipments can, in the United States, also move from a port of entry to a zone without triggering charges and inspection.

2.3.5. Insurance benefits

Customs supervision of zones may lead to lower security costs and reduced insurance costs; in the case of insurance, as duties are not paid, they do not figure in the calculation of the value of the insured good (Ferguson and Steverango, 2013[32]).

2.3.6. Infrastructure

Zones are likely to be located in strategic ports of entry, and they have often benefitted from targeted government infrastructure upgrades, particularly in developing countries that have made zone development a priority. Moreover, jurisdictions may seek to attract investment through supporting site, facilities and equipment development, as well as workforce training (Ferguson and Steverango, 2013[32]).

2.3.7. Working conditions

Special regimes may exist with respect to rules and regulations governing working conditions; these may or may not serve the interests of workers. Use of foreign labour, for example, is sometimes facilitated, and special conditions may apply. In the case of Panama, some, but not all zones have regimes which prescribe: i) a fixed surcharge of 25 per cent for overtime work; ii) flexibility to assign days off, iii) flexibility to operate on Sundays and holidays, and iv) the possibility to terminate labour contracts because of market or demand changes (Pancanada, 2017[33]).

2.3.8. Bulk-breaking, packaging and labelling

Zones provide a platform where goods can be handled and prepared for shipment to different markets, while preserving duty-free status (Ferguson and Steverango, 2013[32]). This can include repackaging and labelling.

2.3.9. Marketing and distribution networks

Zones can represent an important platform for businesses to enhance their distribution and commercial networks, especially in countries where zones are primarily a mechanism for boosting exports. The Colón Free Zone in Panama is a case in point (Box 2.3).

Box 2.3. Colón Free Zone

The Colón Free Zone (CFZ) in Panama, established in 1948, is the second largest in the world; it is managed by the government. In 2015, more than 2 500 merchants, employing close to 30 000 workers, operated in the zone, which is strategically located on the Atlantic Ocean, near the Panama Canal. Operations permitted in the zone include i) importation and export of goods ii) manufacturing, iii) sale, commercialization and distribution of goods and iv) the refining and processing of goods. In 2015, imports topped USD 10 billion; the leading sources were China (33%), Singapore (26%) and the United States (10%). Europe and other Asian economies accounted for another 12% and 9%, respectively. Re-exports reached USD 11.4 billion; the top destinations were American countries (99%), led by Puerto Rico (21%), Colombia (13%), Venezuela (12%) and Panama itself (10%). Value-added in zone operations was on the order USD 1 billion.

Source: (Haussman, Obach and Santos, 2016[23]).

On the supply side, Asian and US exporters shipping to American markets are often interested in shipping large containers of like products. Using the CFZ, they can sell to one merchant in the zone, with the expectation that their products will then be distributed and retailed throughout Central and South America and the Caribbean (ITA, 2016[34]). The distribution is facilitated by the many buyers who travel to the zone with an interest in filling containers with smaller quantities of a broad range of goods (Moore Stephens International, 2006).

2.3.10. Administrative accommodations

Streamlined administrative procedures including "one-stop" services to support businesses setting up in zones and a relatively light regulatory environment can provide further incentives for businesses to locate in zones. In the case of the United Arab Emirates (Petch, 2017[35]; UAE Government, 2017[36]) for example:

- Unlike businesses located in the UAE customs territory, which require a local partner with majority ownership if the business needs a commercial or industrial license to operate, business in in zones can be 100% foreign owned.
- The approach to paperwork is simplified; less documentation is required when setting up and running a company in zones and much of the documentation is available in English.
- Share capital requirements can be low or even non-existent; moreover, there are no capital requirements if the zone operation is a branch of an existing firm.
- Some zones do not require much, if any, physical office space (residency, however, may be required)
- Visas for family and employees are relatively quick and easy to get for zone residents.
- While annual audits may be mandatory, in some cases none are required.

Moreover, an individual can establish a one-person enterprise as a "freelancer" in a zone in the United Arab Emirates, further cutting down on administrative requirements.

The ability of this more relaxed regulatory environment to address key corporate governance matters was questioned in (FATF, 2010[37]). The report notes that important laws and regulations that are applied within the customs territories are often not applied in zones, Anti-Money Laundering/ Combating Financing of Terrorism (AML/CFT) regulations being a case in point. Inadequate control by customs agencies was seen as potentially raising problems in the fields of intellectual property, supply chain security, valuation fraud and other non-fiscal offences. And there were concerns over the lack of sufficient oversight of firms forming companies to operate in zones. Many zone authorities, it was noted, operate separate company formation services from those that exist in the rest of the jurisdiction, and they market the ease of setting up a legal entity in an FTZ to attract business; these authorities often request little or no ownership information on the companies interested in setting up operations in the zone.

2.3.11. Trade measures

Goods that are subject to quotas or are barred from direct entry into a country's home market may nonetheless be admitted for entry, storage and/or manipulation in a zone. In such instances, companies importing goods under quota could eventually either i) hold the goods in the zone until such time as new entries were permitted under the quota, ii) export the goods to foreign markets or iii) use the goods in the zone to produce new items that were not subject to quotas, thereby making them eligible for import into the customs territory of the host country. By the same token, it might be possible, in certain instances, for processers/manufacturers in the zone to use prohibited goods imported into zones to produce new items that can then be shipped to the host country's domestic market.

There may also be instances where products subject to dumping, subsidy and safeguard remedies can be imported freely into zones, without being subject to those measures. In these instances, as above, i) goods could be exported to foreign markets freely and ii) the goods imported into the zones could be used to produce new items that were not subject to the trade remedies, thereby making possible their import on more liberal terms.

References

Blanco de Armas, E. and M. Sadni-Jallap (2002), *A Review of the Role and Impact of Export Processing Zones in World Trade: the Case of Mexico*, GATE Working Paper 2002-07, CNRS, Écully, https://halshs.archives-ouvertes.fr/halshs-00178444/docu.

Bolle, M. and B. Williams (2013), *U.S. Foreign-Trade Zones: Background and Issues for Congress, Congressional Research Service,*, https://fas.org/sgp/crs/misc/R42686.pdf.

Boyenge, J. (2007), *ILO Database on Export Processing Zones (Revised)*, Working Paper 271, International Labour Office, Geneva.

British American Business (2017), *US Foreign-Trade Zones Offer an Attractive Harbour for Global Companies*, American British Trade and Investment, London, http://tradeinvest.babinc.org/ambrit/practical-advice/foreign-trade-zones (accessed on 9 December 2017).

DP World (2018), *http://web.dpworld.com/*.

Engman, M., O. Onodera and E. Pinali (2007), "Export Processing Zones: Past and Future Role in Trade and Development", *OECD Trade Policy Papers*, No. 53, OECD Publishing, Paris, http://dx.doi.org/10.1787/035168776831.

Farole, T. and G. Akinci (2011), *Special Economic Zones : Progress, Emerging Challenges, and Future Directions*, World Bank, Washington, DC, https://openknowledge.worldbank.org/handle/10986/2341.

FATF (2010), *Money Laundering Vulnerabilities of Free Trade Zones*, FATF/OECD, Paris, http://www.fatf-gafi.org/media/fatf/documents/reports/ML%20vulnerabilities%20of%20Free%20Trade%20Zones.pdf.

Ferguson, M. and C. Steverango (2013), *Maximizing the Potential of the Foreign Trade Zone Concept in Canada, McMaster Institute for Transportation and Logistics*, McMaster University, Hamilton, http://mitl.mcmaster.ca/reports/MITL_FTZ_Report.pdf.

Foreign-Trade Zones Board (2016), *77th Annual Report of the Foreign-Trade Zones Board to the Congress of the United States*, Foreign-Trade Zones Board, Springfield, http://enforcement.trade.gov/ftzpage/annualreport/ar-2015.pdf.

Foreign-Trade Zones Resource Center (2017), *Foreign-Trade Zone Benefits*, http://www.foreign-trade-zone.com/benefits.htm (accessed on 9 December 2017).

GAO (1984), *Foreign-Trade Zones Growth Primarily Benefits Users Who Import for Domestic Commerce*, GAO/GGD 84-52, United States General Accounting Office, Gaithersburg, http://www.gao.gov/assets/150/141214.pdf.

GAO (1989), *Foreign-Trade Zones Program Needs Clarified Criteria*, GAO/NSAID-89-85, United States General Accounting Office, Gaithersburg, http://www.gao.gov/assets/150/147348.pdf.

Hainsworth, J. (2017), *Secret foreign trade zone benefits every shipper must know*, The Calgary Region, Canada, http://www.investcalgaryregion.ca/blog/secret-foreign-trade-zone-benefits-shippers-must-know (accessed on 9 December 2017).

Hainsworth, J. (2017), *What is a foreign trade zone and how your business can benefit.*, The Calgary Region, Canada, http://www.investcalgaryregion.ca/blog/ foreign-trade-zone-how-your-business-can-benefit (accessed on 9 December 2017).

Haussman, R., J. Obach and M. Santos (2016), *Special Economic Zones in Panama: Technology Spillovers from a Labor Market Perspective*, Center for International Development Working Paper, Harvard University, https://growthlab.cid.harvard.edu/files/growthlab/files/sez_panama_wp_326.pdf.

ILO (2014), *Trade Union Manual on Export Processing Zones*, International Labour Organization, Geneva, http://www.ilo.org/wcmsp5/groups/public/---ed_dialogue/---actrav/documents/publication/wcms_324632.pdf.

ITA (2016), *Sell Through Panama's Colon Free Trade Zone to the Region – A U.S. Export Opportunity*, The International Trade Administration, U.S. Department of Commerce, https://2016.export.gov/PANAMA/doingbusinessinpanama/exportingtolatinamericathroughpanama/index.asp.

Jafza (2017), *Jebel Ali Freezone*, http://jafza.ae.

Jayanthakumaran, K. (2003), "Benefit-Cost Appraisals of Export Processing Zones: A Survey of the Literature", *Development Policy Review*, Vol. 21/1, pp. 51-65.

Pancanada (2017), *Panama as Headquarters for Canadian Multinationals*, Panama-Canada Chamber of Commerce, http://www.pancanada.org/wp-content/uploads/2014/07/Panama-as-Headquarters-for-Canadian-Multinationals-modelo-2-2014.pdf [(accessed on 9 December 2017).

Papadopoulus, N. and S. Malhotra (2007), "Export Processing Zones in Development and International Marketing: An Integrative Review and Research Agenda", *Journal of Macromarketing*, Vol. 27/2, http://dx.doi.org/10.1177/0276146707300070.

Petch, N. (2017), *Nine reasons for entrepreneurs to set up in UAE free zones*, Virtuzone, http://vz.ae/2017/01/26/nine-reasons-entrepreneurs-set-uae-free-trade-zones/ (accessed on 9 December 2017).

U.S. Customs and Border Protection (2017), *User fee - Merchandise Processing Fees*, https://help.cbp.gov/app/answers/detail/a_id/334/~/user-fee---merchandise-processing-fees.

UAE Government (2017), *Starting a business in a free zone*, The Official Portal of the UAE Government, https://government.ae/en/information-and-services/business/starting-a-business-in-a-free-zone (accessed on 9 December 2017).

UNCTAD (2002), *World Investment Report 2002: Transnational Corporations and Export Competitiveness*, United Nations Conference on Trade and Development, Geneva, http://unctad.org/en/docs/wir2002_en.pdf.

UNCTAD (2013), *World Investment Report 2013_Global Value Chains: Investment and Trade for Development*, United Nations Conference on Trade and Development, Geneva, http://unctad.org/en/PublicationsLibrary/wir2013_en.pdf.

UNCTAD (2015), *Enhancing the Contribution of Export Processing Zones to the Sustainable Development Goals: An analysis of 100 EPZs and a Framework for Sustainable Economic Zones*, United Nations Conference on Trade and Development, Geneva, http://unctad.org/en/PublicationsLibrary/wir2013_en.pdf.

USITC (1984), *The Implications of Foreign Trade Zones for U.S. Industries and for Competitive Conditions Between U.S. and Foreign Firms*, USITC publication 1496, United States International Trade Commission, Washington, http://www.usitc.gov/publications/332/pub1496.pdf.

USITC (1988), *The Implications of Foreign Trade Zones for U.S. Industries and for Competitive Conditions Between U.S. and Foreign Firms*, USITC publication 2059, United States International Trade Commission, Washington, http://www.usitc.gov/publications/332/pub1496.pdf.

Wikipedia Contributors (2017), *Foreign-trade zones of the United States*, Wikipedia, The Free Encyclopedia, https://en.wikipedia.org/wiki/Foreign-trade_zones_of_the_United_States (accessed on 9 December 2017).

World Bank (2017), *Special Economic Zones : An Operational Review of Their Impacts*, World Bank, Washington, DC, https://openknowledge.worldbank.org/handle/10986/29054.

3. FTZs and trade in fakes: Empirical evidence

Free Trade Zones can provide a range of advantages to countries that host them and to businesses that operate in these zones. However, light regulation applied to zones' operations can attract parties engaged in illegal and criminal activities. Existing governance gaps can provide rogue operators with a relatively safe environment in which to carry out their illicit activities. Consequently, FTZs can facilitate trade in counterfeit and pirated products, as well as smuggling and money laundering.

This chapter is intended to shed light on whether there is evidence to indicate that the existence of FTZs may result in a higher rate of counterfeiting activities and piracy. In other words, it aims to estimate the extent to which the existence, number and size of FTZs increase the value of counterfeit and pirated products exported by a given economy. While relevant, this exercise is particularly challenging.

Firstly, precise data on FTZs and counterfeiting and piracy by economy are scarce. This study, however, takes advantage of recent major advances in research on these two respective areas. Data on FTZs are mainly extracted from the World FTZ Database (2014), which brings together data from hundreds of academic resources, published papers and books, reports by international organisations, and documents on specific regions, countries and zones (Yücer, Siroën and Archanskaia, 2014[38]). Data on counterfeiting and piracy is based on the recent OECD-EUIPO (2016) study, which employed an innovative methodology that made it possible to gauge the value of global counterfeit and pirated trade by provenance economy worldwide (OECD/EUIPO, 2016[39]). Both sources are presented in detail in the following subsections.

Secondly, factors other than FTZs may encourage traffickers to engage in counterfeiting and smuggling activities. Reliable estimates of the extent to which the existence and/or the size of FTZs affect the export value of counterfeit and pirated products can be obtained only by neutralising the impact of these external factors (i.e. "all other things being equal"). For this purpose, a proper econometric methodology has to be developed. The chapter will therefore first present the data and the required methodology before turning to the results.

3.1. Data on FTZs and counterfeiting activities

3.1.1. Data on FTZs

Information on national FTZ policy and activity was extracted from two different sources. The first one is the World FTZ database (Yücer, Siroën and Archanskaia, 2014[38]), which contains detailed information on the number and size of FTZs across economies worldwide. The second source is the PRONTO database (PRONTO, 2017[40]), which, as compared to the first one, do not include such detailed information but allows instead distinguishing between the different types of EPZs that are "pure" export processing zones (EPZs), export and import processing zones (EMPZs) and special economic zones (SEZs).

World FTZ database

The primarily source for data on FTZ is the World FTZ Database (Yücer, Siroën and Archanskaia, 2014[38]), which synthesises information about FTZ programs in 158 countries. The definition of FTZs is quite restrictive, as limited specifically to EPZs.

In this database, EPZs are defined as zones with an export processing activity, which are (i) based on a transformation of imported inputs and, (ii) benefit from tariff exemptions under specific conditions that differentiate beneficiary firms from non-beneficiary firms. For example, free ports, transit zones, "duty free" zones and zones eligible for other incentives excluding tariff exemptions were excluded.

In an individual file made available for each economy, the World FTZ database presents the countries' number of EPZs, characteristics, locations, years of implementation, size, fiscal regulations, industrial specialisations etc.

These data were initially informed by both the WTO Trade Policy Reviews, written by the WTO Secretariat, and by the Investment Climate Statements published by the US Department of State (Yücer, Siroën and Archanskaia, 2014[38]). These two resources indeed systematically provide information on national FTZ policy and activities. The database also draws from academic resources, published papers and books, reports by international organisations such as the United Nations and the World Bank, and information on specific regions, countries and zones.

In order to enhance the robustness of the results obtained in the following empirical exercise, this study has also called upon information from an alternative data source on FTZs, the PRONTO database (PRONTO, 2017[40]). While the World FTZ database does indeed provide very rich information on the size of FTZs (i.e. number of firms, value of exports, or employment), many countries observed in this database are associated with at least one EPZ. If the existence of EPZs is treated as a dummy variable only, this could potentially cause a lack of variance in the data.

The advantage of the PRONTO (2017)[40] database is that it distinguishes between three types of EPZs. The first of these are "pure" EPZs defined as designated areas where firms can import goods duty free for further processing and re-export (PRONTO, 2015[41]). In those EPZs, firms can also export to the domestic market, but in this case they must also pay import duties on the goods sold domestically.

A second set of free trade zones are export and import processing zones (EMPZs), which allow for preferential (even duty free) sale to the domestic market from inside designated areas that otherwise function like EPZs.

A final set of zones are special economic zones (SEZs) that, while not focused specifically on exports, nonetheless provide a mix of preferential tax treatment, lower regulatory burdens and preferred access to infrastructure services. Such zones are sometimes designed to attract foreign investment or encourage domestic investment in certain regions or sectors.

Under the hypothesis that economies with dominant "pure" EPZs as defined in the PRONTO database may be more prone to ship fakes, since customs officials there have fewer incentives to check goods which are less likely to end up in their own territories, it would stand to reason that economies registered as having EPZs would tend to exhibit greater values of counterfeit and pirated exports.

Overview of FTZ data

The unified database on FTZ created from the World FTZ and PRONTO databases covers 134 economies worldwide (Table 3.1). Among them, 101 economies (75%) are reported as having at least one EPZ in the World FTZ database, while 85 economies (56%) are reported as having at least one "pure" EPZ, SEZ or EMPZ in the PRONTO database.

One of the important insights of Table 3.1 is that FTZs are found throughout the world and are present in both developed and developing economies. In addition, "pure" EPZs are the most widespread type of zones in all continents, as compared to EMPZs and SEZs.

Table 3.1. Number of economies with at least one FTZ (EPZ, SEZ and EMPZ)

Number of economies with at least one:	EPZ[2] (World FTZ database)	EPZ[3], SEZ[4] or EMPZ[5] (PRONTO)	EPZ (PRONTO)	EMPZ (PRONTO)	SEZ (PRONTO)
Africa (31)[1]	23	19	16	3	4
Asia (23)	17	15	13	2	8
Middle East (11)	9	7	6	2	1
North America and Caribbean (10)	7	7	5	1	1
Central America (7)	7	7	7	0	2
South America (11)	8	10	8	2	0
Europe (37)	27	7	4	0	4
Oceania (4)	3	3	2	0	1
World (134)	**101**	**75**	**61**	**10**	**21**

Notes: 1) Figures in parenthesis are the total number of economies for each at least one information about FTZ activities is reported in the database by continent. 2) The World FTZ database defines EPZs as zones with export processing activities, which are (i) based on a transformation of imported inputs and, (ii) benefit from tariff exemptions under specific conditions that differentiate beneficiary firms from non-beneficiary firms. 3) In the PRONTO database, EPZs are defined as designated areas where firms can import goods duty free for further processing and re-export. 4) In the PRONTO database, EMPZs are defined as free trade zones that allow for preferential (even duty free) sale to the domestic market from inside designated areas, that otherwise function like EPZs. 5) In the PRONTO database, SEZs are defined as zones that provide a mix of preferential tax treatment, lower regulatory burdens and preferred access to infrastructure services while not focused specifically on production for export.

Sources: (Yücer, Siroën and Archanskaia, 2014[38]; PRONTO, 2015[41]; PRONTO, 2017[40]).A detailed analysis of the data provided by the World FTZ database reveals that 1843 FTZs can be found worldwide, and that almost half of these zones are located in Asia (Table 3.2). The number of zones reported at the global level is less important than more cited references (>3000) for two main reasons. First, not all countries are covered by the database. Second, given the restrictive definition of FTZs within the database (only EPZs) some zones, such as zones only devoted to transit, storage and transhipment, were excluded.

The global value of exports from EPZs is USD 3500 billion, which represent 29% of total exports of economies included in the World FTZ database. Exporting more than USD 2400 billion from EPZs, around 42% of their total exports, Asian economies are clearly the front runners. They are followed by Middle East economies (USD 552 billion, 55% of exports) and South American economies (USD 284 billion, 55% of exports). The value of exports from EPZs is lower for African and Central American economies (USD 64 and

10 billion, respectively), but their intensity is still quite high (this corresponds to 24% and 29% of their total exports, respectively). Finally and importantly, these statistics show a number of outliers – economies for which a large number of zones does not necessarily translate in a large volumes and/or intensity of exports from EPZs. This is the case for Europe, North America and Caribbean, as well as Oceania.

Comprising 70%, 9% and 6% of the 21 million of employees working in EPZs throughout the world, Asia, Central America and Middle East, respectively, appear also as front runners in terms of employment within EPZs, This is consistent with the recent findings of ILO (2014)[6], although the total number of employees in FTZs estimated in ILO's report is larger (35 millions). As for the case of exports, this is related to differences in country coverage, and in definition of FTZs (see above).

Table 3.2. Summary statistics on FTZs

Continent	Number of zones	Exports from EPZs[1] (in USD bn)	Share of exports from EPZ[2]	Number of employees in EPZs (in thousand)	Number of firms in EPZs
Africa	154	64	24.0%	1650	8274
Asia	802	2400	42.4%	14956	68637
Middle-East	123	522	55.1%	1083	17159
Europe	122	179	6.9%	716	17558
North America and Caribbean	335	39	2.5%	523	3878
Central America	246	10	29.0%	1893	7502
South America	46	284	54.8%	386	9640
Oceania	15	1	0.2%	34	301
World	**1843**	**3500**	**28.9%**	**21241**	**132889**

Notes: 1) EPZs are defined here as zones with export processing activities, which are (i) based on a transformation of imported inputs and, (ii) benefit from tariff exemptions under specific conditions that differentiate beneficiary firms from non-beneficiary firms. 2) The shares of exports from EPZs were calculated only over the total exports of economies for which information on FTZ activity was available in the database.
Source: Authors' own calculations based on the World FTZ database Yücer, Siroën and Archanskaia, 2014[38]

3.1.2. Data on counterfeit and pirated trade

All information concerning counterfeit and pirated trade comes from the OECD-EUIPO (2016) database on customs seizures. This resource brings together data from three separate datasets from the WCO, the DG TAXUD of the European Commission and the US Department of Homeland Security (OECD/EUIPO, 2016[39]). The database includes detailed information on seizures of IPR-infringing goods made by customs officers in 99 economies around the world between 2011 and 2013. For each year, there are more than 100 000 observations in the database; in most cases, each individual observation corresponds to one customs seizure.

The database contains a wealth of information about the IPR-infringing goods, data that can be used for quantitative and qualitative analysis. In most cases, for each seizure the database details: the date of seizure, the mode of transport of the fake products, the departure and destination economies, the general statistical category of the goods seized and a detailed description of the goods, the name of legitimate brand owner, the number of products seized and their approximate value[1].

Based on this database on customs seizures of IP-infringing products, the OECD-EUIPO (2016) study developed a methodology, the General Trade-Related Index of Counterfeiting (GTRIC), which made it possible to measure the value of global trade in counterfeit and pirated goods (OECD/EUIPO, 2016[39]). The GTRIC methodology has also made it possible both to identify the key provenance economies for counterfeit imports around the world and to produce estimates as to the ceiling values of counterfeit and pirated products globally imported from those economies.

Table 3.3 below reports the (estimated) value of counterfeit and pirated exports by continent for 2013, and in reports these values in detail by provenance economy for the period 2011-2013. As mentioned in OECD/EUIPO (2016)[39], international trade in counterfeit and pirated products represented up to 2.5% of world trade in 2013, or as much as USD 461 billion. Asian economies are the largest exporter of counterfeit and pirated goods in terms of value, with USD 310 billion of fake exports (Table 3.3).

In relative terms, Asian, Middle East and African economies are the largest exporters of counterfeit and pirated products. The estimated share of world exports of fake goods in provenance of Asia is indeed the highest (5.3%), followed by those in provenance of Middle East (2.4%) and Africa (1.6%).

Table 3.3. Exports of counterfeit and pirated goods, by continents, 2013

Continent	Value in USD billion	Share of exports[*]
Africa	6	1.6%
Asia	310	5.3%
Middle-East	29	2.4%
Europe	83	1.2%
North America and Caribbean	23	1.1%
Central America	5	1.1%
South America	5	0.9%
Oceania	1	0.4%
World	**461**	**2.5%**

Note: *Share of counterfeit and pirated exports were calculated over the total value exports from economies for which information on the value of counterfeit and pirated trade was available.
Source: Authors' own calculations based on OECD/EUIPO (2016).

Two factors are especially worth bearing in mind when considering these figures. First, the term "ceiling value" is crucial in this context, as it refers to the upper boundary of counterfeit imports from each of these economies. Second, these amounts do not include (i) domestically produced and consumed counterfeit and pirated products or (ii) digital piracy via the Internet.

3.1.3. Simple correlations between FTZs and counterfeiting activities

A first look at correlations between the estimated value of counterfeit and pirated products exported from each provenance economy and FTZs-related variables provides interesting insights. Firstly, the number of FTZs within an economy (as reported in the World FTZ database) seem to be correlated with the value of its exports of counterfeit and pirated products, even though there is a number of outliers – economies for which a large number of zones does not necessarily translate into large volumes of fake exports (Figure 3.1). This finding shows a large variability in zones performance in terms of trade in fake goods.

It also follows the basic fact that FTZs tend to differ to a large scale among themselves, which manifests in different degrees of oversight and compliance with enforcement authorities. A relevant example is the United States, where a large number of zones does not result in a large flow of fake goods, partially due to a sound compliance and oversight systems (see Box 3.1).

Figure 3.1. Number of FTZs and value of counterfeit and pirated exports, 2013

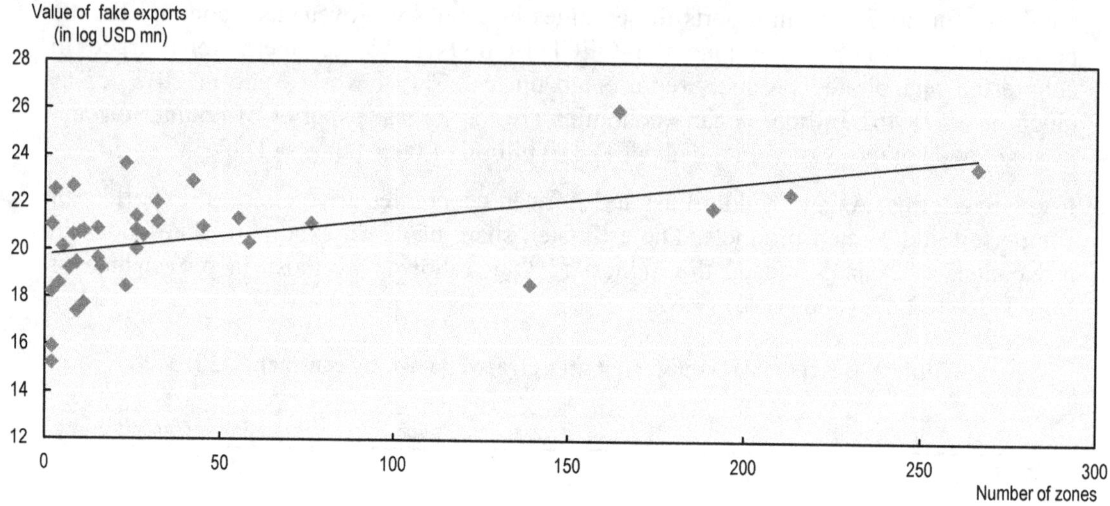

Sources: (OECD/EUIPO, 2016[39]); (Yücer, Siroën and Archanskaia, 2014[38])

Box 3.1. Free Trade Zones in the United States

The US FTZ program was established in 1934. It provides tariff benefits and facilitated customs-entry procedures to promote investment, US manufacturing and distribution, employment, and exports. Today it comprises over 230 zones and nearly 400 subzones in all 50 US States and Puerto Rico. The main industries active in zones include automotive, pharmaceuticals and ICTs. Remarkably, these industries are prone to counterfeiting, as demonstrated by the OECD-EUIPO (2016) study.

The FTZs system in the US was designed to support effective controls of activities and flows to FTZs and improve collection, storage, and access to reliable and comprehensive customs statistics on incoming or outgoing goods and on production of goods and services inside them. It does so by imposing higher compliance requirements on zone operators than regular importers and closer and more frequent interaction with the US Customs and Border Protection agency (CBP).

For example, before production in a zone can be approved for activation, an operator must file with CBP an Application for Activation and Procedures and Operations Manual describing internal compliance processes and goods moving through the zone or subzone. CBP must then approve the Application and Manual. It conducts a physical review of the facilities, undertakes a background check of key employees, and reviews activities to be conducted in the zone. CBP's oversight of FTZ operations is done on a risk-based, audit-inspection system rather than through on-site supervision by CBP personnel. Compliance is assured through compliance reviews (i.e. audits) and spot checks.

Source: US National Association of Foreign-Trade Zones (NAFTZ)

Not only the number but also the total size of FTZs within an economy seems to be correlated with the value of its exports of counterfeit and pirated products. To illustrate this, Figure 3.2 plots the relationship between the value of fakes exported from each provenance economy in 2013 and their respective (a) number of firms operating in EPZs; (b) number of employees working in EPZs; and (c) value of exports made from EPZs.

Clearly, the larger the number of firms and employees in a country's EPZs, and the greater the value of exports from the zones, the larger the value of counterfeit and pirated products exported from the country's economy. In other words, the larger the size of EPZs within an economy, the more this economy appears to be a potential source of counterfeit and pirated products in global trade.

The relationship between FTZ-related variables and counterfeiting activities plotted in Figure 3.2 is even more striking considering that the two types of data come from two completely different sources (see Sections 3.1.1 and Section 3.1.2). In order to confirm these correlations and to provide a robust quantitative analysis, the following subsection sets out an econometric model that makes it possible to come to an accurate estimate of how the existence, size or number of FTZs affect the value of counterfeit and pirated exports from a given economy, taking other relevant factors into account as well.

Figure 3.2. Size of FTZs and value of fake exports by provenance economy, 2013

(a) Number of firms operating in EPZs

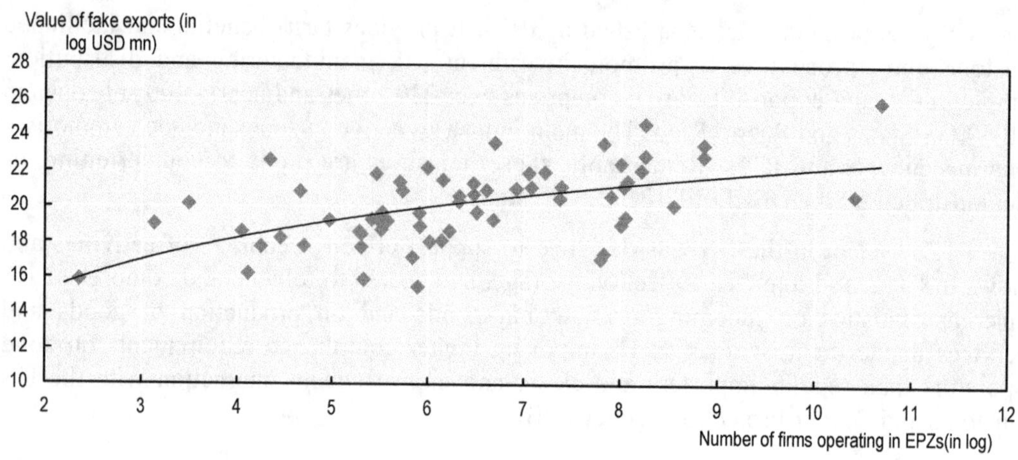

(b) Employment in EPZs

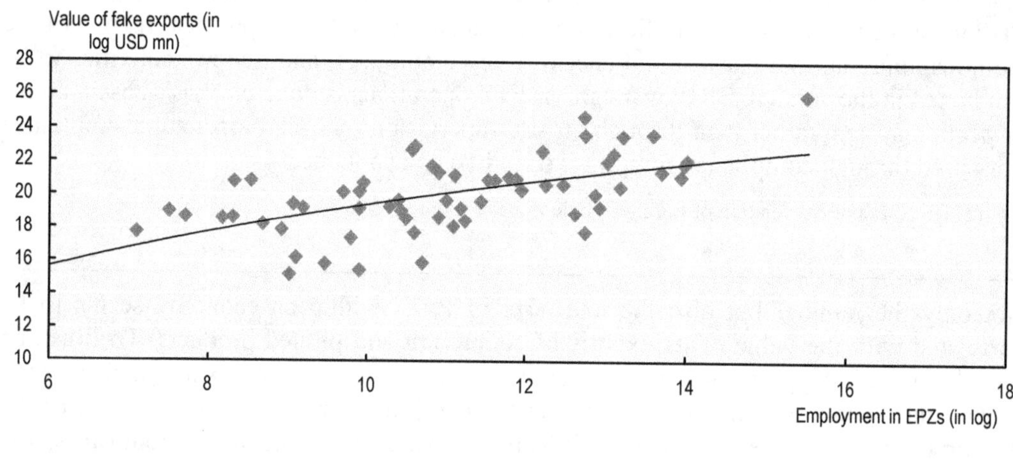

(c) Exports from EPZs

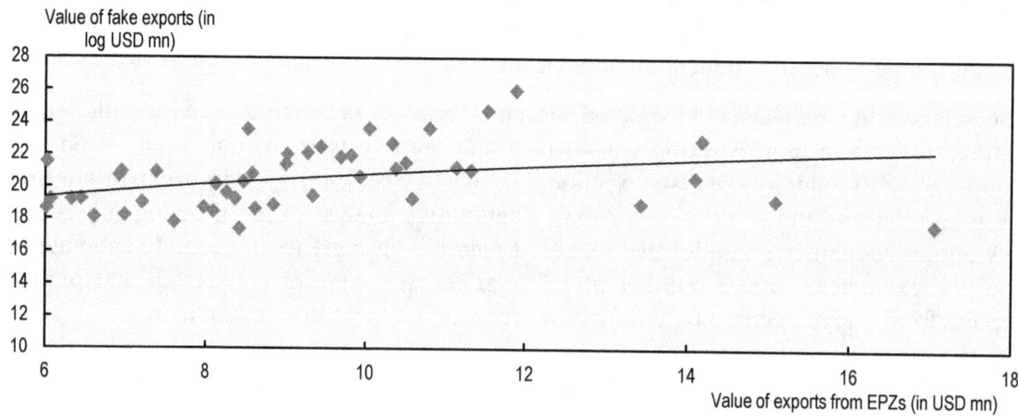

Sources: (OECD/EUIPO, 2016[39]); (Yücer, Siroën and Archanskaia, 2014[38])

3.2. FTZs and trade in counterfeit and pirated goods: Methodology

3.2.1. Factors influencing trade in counterfeit and pirated goods

The purpose of this exercise is to determine whether FTZs encourage traffickers to engage into counterfeiting and piracy. More precisely, the aim here is to estimate the extent to which the existence, number and size of FTZs increase the value of counterfeit and pirated products exported by a given economy. However, other factors also encourage traffickers to export counterfeit and pirated products, so other control variables should be used in this equation.

The first control variable used for the purposes of this study is the ***GDP per capita*** of the provenance economies (in current USD), data taken from the World Bank (2017)[42] database. The OECD/EUIPO (2016)[39] study provided a strong indication that the propensity of an economy to be the source of counterfeit and pirated goods in international trade was related to its income level.

More specifically, there seems to be a relationship between the propensity of economies to export counterfeit and pirated products to the global market and their GDP per capita, with the association taking the form of an inverted U shape. Low-income economies generally lack the capital and technological capacity to produce a wide range of products, which also limits their capability to produce infringing goods. As economies develop and grow richer, so do their productive and technological capabilities, which affects the possibility for higher scale infringement activities. Institutional developments (including the adoption of IP-related legislation and enforcement practices) tend to lag behind economic development, which creates favourable conditions for infringement activities. As economies grow still richer and become more knowledge-based, greater emphasis is placed on the role of IP, and legislation and enforcement in these areas is tightened through improved public governance.

In light of the differences observed between countries in terms of their governance structure, this study also used as a control variable the scores on a perception-based index rating the ***control of corruption*** within each provenance economy. This indicator is provided by the World Bank (Kaufmann, Kraay and Mastruzzi, 2010[42]) and is based on several hundred individual variables measuring perceptions of corruptions drawn from 31 separate data sources constructed by 25 different organizations. The particular aspect of corruption measured by the various sources differs somewhat, ranging from the frequency of "additional payments to get things done", to the effects of corruption on the business environment. Estimate gives the country's score on the aggregate indicator, in units of a standard normal distribution, i.e. ranging from approximately -2.5 to 2.5, with higher scores corresponding to better outcomes. Therefore, if a higher level of corruption do create a favourable conditions for infringements activities, it would be expected that the value of world imports of counterfeit and pirated products from a given provenance economy would decrease as a function of its control of corruption indicator.

A country's capacity to export fakes is also expected to vary according to the economy's overall export capacity. ***Export volumes*** from each provenance economy are therefore also used as additional control variables. The data are taken from the well-known UN Comtrade database (United Nations Statistics Division, 2017[43]). Finally, and with the same reasoning, the average ***time to export*** (in days) for each economy also serves as additional dependant variable. These data were extracted from the CEPII (2017)[44] Gravity Database.

3.2.2. Model

An econometric specification is used to calculate whether the existence, the number or the size of FTZs in a given economy significantly increase the value of counterfeit and pirated goods exported from that economy. For this purpose, a linear econometric model, which expresses the value of counterfeit and pirated goods exported from each economy as a function of FTZ-related variables and other control variables, is used as follows:

$$\ln C_{it} = \alpha + \ln X_i + \ln Z_{it} + \delta_t + \varepsilon_{it} \qquad \textbf{Equation 3.1}$$

In Equation 3.1, C_{it} is the estimated value of fakes exported from each provenance economy i in year t (see Section 3.1.2). These data are available from 2011 to 2013. X_i represents the FTZ-related variables for each provenance economy. They include: a dummy variable for the existence of EPZs, which equals 1 when the provenance economy has at least one EPZ in its territory, and 0 otherwise; the number of EPZs in the provenance economy; the value of exports via EPZs from each provenance economy; and the number of people employed in those EPZs. All these data are observable once and come from the Dauphine's World FTZ database (see Section 3.1.1).

Z_{it} represents the control variables that also influence the capacity of an economy to export fake products. They include: the provenance economy's GDP per capita, the governance indicator measure its control of corruption; the country's export volume; and the average time to export (see Section 3.2.1).

δ_t are time fixed-effect terms to control for common factors between all provenance economies that might influence global trade in counterfeit and pirated products each year. This could refer to, for example, the overall condition of the global economy in a given year that in turn impacts the volumes of trade, including trade in fakes. Finally, α is a constant and ε_{it} are the residuals of Equation 3.1.

In order to not exclude observations with zero, and thus to avoid any biases, variables were only log-transformed when their value was larger than 0; while 0 was assigned to all cases where the variables were equal to 0 in level. In addition, "robust" standard errors were used to obtain unbiased standard errors of coefficients in Equation 3.1, as heteroscedasticity was suspected. Note that results commented in the following subsection are also robust to the clustering of observations at the country level.

Finally, endogeneity tests were performed for each specification whose results are displayed in the following section. In the case analysed here, endogeneity could have occurred as a result of measurement errors, simultaneous causality[2] or omitted variables in Equation 3.1. However, endogeneity tests were performed for each FTZs-related variable and all concluded that there is no problem of endogeneity in the model. The results commented below are therefore robust.

3.3. Results

In order to statistically verify the relationship between FTZs and fake exports presented in Figure 3.2, Equation 3.1 was run over the full sample of provenance economies for the period 2011-2013. The results are displayed in Table 3.4 and Table 3.5 below, using alternative independent FTZ-related variables. Given the existence of some outliers in the sample for which the value of exports counterfeit and pirated of products is very large as compared to other economies, Equation 3.1 was also run leaving China and Hong Kong

(China) out of the analysis. Results are displayed in Table A.2 and in the annex and confirm that the outcomes commented below are robust to the exclusion of outliers.

3.3.1. Existence, number and type of FTZs and trade in fake goods

Columns (1) and (2) of display the results of the estimations using dummies of EPZs as independent variables (column (1) is based on the World FTZ database, column (2) on the PRONTO database; see Section 3.1.1). Clearly, the existence of at least one EPZ within an economy significantly increases the value of counterfeit and pirated products exported from that economy.

Column (3) tests the same relationship using dummies for the different types of FTZs available in the PRONTO database ("pure" EPZs, EMPZs, SEZs; see Section 3.1.1). Note that each provenance economy can be recorded as having none, only one, two or the three types of zones within its territory. Interestingly, the results show that only "pure" EPZs are significantly associated with a larger value of counterfeit and pirated exports. This result follows the fact that, compared to EMPZs and SEZs, "pure" EPZs are more prone to ship fakes, as customs officials there have fewer incentives to check goods which are less likely to end up in their own territories. It then naturally stands to reason that economies registered as having EPZs exhibit greater values of counterfeit and pirated exports.

Moving beyond the existence and type of EPZs, column (4) tests whether the number of EPZs is a significant determinant of the value of counterfeit and pirated goods exported by an economy. It shows that an additional EPZ within an economy is associated with, on average, a significant increase of 5.9% in the value of fake goods exported from that economy. This means that the larger the number of EPZs within an economy, the more likely it is to be a provenance economy for counterfeit and pirated products in global trade.

Table 3.4. Existence, number of FTZs and exports of counterfeit and pirated products, 2011-2013

	Dependant variable: value of counterfeit and pirated exports (in log) by economy and year			
	(1)	(2)	(3)	(4)
Export value (in log)	0.825***	0.782***	0.789***	0.829***
	(0.098)	(0.090)	(0.090)	(0.083)
GDP per capita (in log)	15.446***	15.629***	15.296***	10.370*
	(5.207)	(5.137)	(5.137)	(5.272)
GDP per capita^2 (in log)	-0.729**	-0.732***	-0.709**	-0.507*
	(0.286)	(0.281)	(0.281)	(0.297)
Control of corruption index	-1.231***	-0.967**	-1.032**	-1.134**
	(0.454)	(0.465)	(0.474)	(0.421)
Time to exports (in days)	-0.131**	-0.143***	-0.143***	-0.189***
	(0.057)	(0.050)	(0.051)	(0.055)
Dummy for EPZ (World FTZ database)	2.505***			
	(0.821)			
Dummy for EPZ (PRONTO)		1.401*		
		(0.761)		
Dummy for pure EPZ (PRONTO)			1.466*	
			(0.783)	

	(1)	(2)	(3)	(4)
Dummy for SEZ (PRONTO)				0.703
				(0.657)
Dummy for EMPZ (PRONTO)				-0.059
				(0.680)
Number of EPZs				0.059**
				(0.025)
_cons	-82.042***	-81.259***	-80.316***	-51.163*
	(23.952)	(23.520)	(23.496)	(26.728)
Observations	336	336	336	258
Adjusted R^2	0.590***	0.573***	0.573***	0.562***
F statistic	39.176 (df= 8; 327)	38.501 (df= 8; 327)	31.051 (df= 10; 325)	30.827 (df= 8; 249)

Notes: Robust standard errors in parentheses. *p<0.1; **p<0.05; ***p<0.01. Estimates are results of Equation 3.1 for the period 2011-2013.

3.3.2. Size of FTZs and trade in fake goods

Moving beyond the existence, the types and the number of EPZs, Table 3.5 tests whether the size of FTZs significantly affects the value of fakes exported from each provenance economy. Column (1) shows that a 1% increase in the value of exports from EPZs within an economy is associated with a significant increase in the value of counterfeit and pirated products exported from that economy, in the amount of 0.28%.

Columns (2) to (3) show that a 1% increase in the number of firms operating in EPZs and in the number of employees working in EPZs within an economy raises the value of counterfeit and pirated exports by 0.29% and 0.21%, respectively. Finally, column (4) shows that an increase of 1% in the value of investments in EPZs raises the value of fake exports by 0.17%.

All these results can lead to the conclusion that the larger the size of the EPZs in an economy, the greater the value of fake products the economy exports globally. This prevails for all types of measures of zones' size available, that is, value of exports from EPZs, employment, investment and number of firms operating in EPZs,

.

Table 3.5. Size of FTZs and exports of counterfeit and pirated products, 2011-2013

	Dependant variable: value of counterfeit and pirated exports (in log) by economy and year			
	(1)	(2)	(3)	(4)
Export value (in log)	0.919***	0.885***	0.903***	0.886***
	(0.085)	(0.099)	(0.103)	(0.110)
GDP per capita (in log)	1.264	14.736**	10.545	3.822
	(7.805)	(7.408)	(7.832)	(7.912)
GDP per capita^2 (in log)	-0.086	-0.733*	-0.520	-0.183
	(0.434)	(0.404)	(0.429)	(0.439)
Control of corruption index	-0.909*	-1.157**	-1.032*	-1.654***
	(0.522)	(0.575)	(0.622)	(0.613)
Time to exports (in days)	-0.300***	-0.197***	-0.217***	-0.326***
	(0.077)	(0.062)	(0.059)	(0.067)
Value of exports from EPZs (in log)	0.284***			
	(0.087)			
Number of firms operating in EPZs (in log)		0.288**		
		(0.141)		
Number of employees in EPZs (in log)			0.205**	
			(0.096)	
Value of investment in EPZs (in log)				0.172***
				(0.057)
_cons	-5.617	-75.106**	-55.038	-18.936
	(34.789)	(34.036)	(35.667)	(35.963)
Observations	183	219	219	180
Adjusted R^2	0.600***	0.547***	0.551***	0.595***
F statistic	29.361 (df= 8; 174)	25.16 (df= 8; 210)	24.394 (df= 8; 210)	22.365 (df= 8; 171)

Notes: Robust standard errors in parentheses. *p<0.1; **p<0.05; ***p<0.01. Estimates are results of Equation 4.1 for the period 2011-2013. All EPZ-related variables are extracted from the World FTZ database (see Section 3.1).

To summarise, the results displayed in and Table 3.5 show a clear relationship between the FTZs in a given economy and trade in counterfeit and pirated goods from that economy. The findings were established taking into account not only the presence of zones, but also their number, type and their size. In all analysed cases zones significantly intensify an economy's counterfeiting activities, notably "pure" EPZs. Their presence in a given economy is likely to result in higher volumes of trade in fakes departing from that economy.

These results are statistically robust, which means they take into account other possible factors that could impact the volumes of trade in counterfeit and pirated goods, such as the overall level of economic development in a given economy, the control of corruption, overall volumes of trade, etc. With all these additional factors taken into consideration, the results remain robust and statistically significant; they indicate that Free Trade Zones have become a useful tool for counterfeiters, who regularly misuse them in their operations

Notes

[1] Concerning valuation of seized goods, there are two principles for reporting the value of counterfeit and pirated goods: 1) declared value (value indicated on customs declarations), which corresponds to values reported in the general trade statistics; and 2) replacement value (price of original goods). The structured interviews with customs officials and the descriptive analysis of values of selected products conducted in OECD-EUIPO (2016) revealed that the declared values are reported in most cases.

[2] Simultaneously bias could have occurred here if the intensity of counterfeiting activities and piracy within an economy led to the creation of FTZs. As mentioned in the main text, endogeneity tests were performed for each FTZs-related variable. They all led to the conclusion that FTZs-related variables were not endogenous, so that there is no problem of reverse causality in the model performed in Section 3.

References

BASCAP (2013), *Controlling the Zone: Balancing facilitation and control to combat illicit trade in the world's Free Trade Zones*, Business Action to Stop Counterfeiting and Piracy, International Chamber of Commerce, Paris, https://cdn.iccwbo.org/content/uploads/sites/3/2016/11/Combating-illicit-trade-in-FTZs-1.pdf.

Blanco de Armas, E. and M. Sadni-Jallap (2002), *A Review of the Role and Impact of Export Processing Zones in World Trade: the Case of Mexico*, GATE Working Paper 2002-07, CNRS, Écully, https://halshs.archives-ouvertes.fr/halshs-00178444/docu.

Bolle, M. and B. Williams (2013), *U.S. Foreign-Trade Zones: Background and Issues for Congress, Congressional Research Service,*, https://fas.org/sgp/crs/misc/R42686.pdf.

Boyenge, J. (2007), *ILO Database on Export Processing Zones (Revised)*, Working Paper 271, International Labour Office, Geneva.

British American Business (2017), *US Foreign-Trade Zones Offer an Attractive Harbour for Global Companies*, American British Trade and Investment, London, http://tradeinvest.babinc.org/ambrit/practical-advice/foreign-trade-zones (accessed on 9 December 2017).

Carribbean Financial Action Task Force (2000), *Money Laundering Prevention Guidelines for CFATF Member Governments, Free Trade Zone Authorities, and Merchants*, http://www.cfatf-gafic.org/index.php/documents/archives/22-free-trade-zone-recommendations-english/file (accessed on 9 December 2017).

CBP (2011), *Foreign-Trade Zones Manual*, US Customs and Border Protection, Department of Homeland Security, http://www.cbp.gov/sites/default/files/documents/FTZmanual2011.pdf.

CEPII (2017), *GRAVITY Database*, http://www.cepii.fr/CEPII/en/bdd_modele/presentation.asp?id=14 (accessed on November 2017).

Chai, Y. and O. Im (2009), *The Development of Free Industrial Zones – The Malaysian Experience*, http://share.nanjing-school.com/dpgeography/files/2012/10/info.worldbank.org-s9hsat.pdf (accessed on 9 December 2017).

Creskoff, S. and P. Walkenhorst (2009), *Implications of WTO Disciplines for Special Economic Zones in Developing Countries,*, Policy Research Working Paper 4892, World Bank, Washington, DC, http://www.researchgate.net/profile/Peter_Walkenhorst/publication/228239934_Implications_of_WTO_Disciplines_for_Special_Economic_Zones_in_Developing_Countries/links/54fd4ee90cf270426d11ca5d/Implications-of-WTO-Disciplines-for-Special-Economic-Zones-in-Developing.

DP World (2018), *http://web.dpworld.com/*.

Engman, M., O. Onodera and E. Pinali (2007), "Export Processing Zones: Past and Future Role in Trade and Development", *OECD Trade Policy Papers*, No. 53, OECD Publishing, Paris, http://dx.doi.org/10.1787/035168776831.

Farole, T. and G. Akinci (2011), *Special Economic Zones : Progress, Emerging Challenges, and Future*

Directions, World Bank, Washington, DC, https://openknowledge.worldbank.org/handle/10986/2341.

FATF (2008), *Best Practices Paper: Best Practices on Trade Based Money Laundering*, FATF/OECD, Paris, http://www.fatf-gafi.org/media/fatf/documents/recommendations/BPP%20Trade%20Based%20Money%20Laundering%202012%20COVER.pdf.

FATF (2010), *Money Laundering Vulnerabilities of Free Trade Zones*, FATF/OECD, Paris, http://www.fatf-gafi.org/media/fatf/documents/reports/ML%20vulnerabilities%20of%20Free%20Trade%20Zones.pdf.

FATF (2012), *International Standards on Combating Money Laundering and the Financing of Terrorism & Proliferation: The FATF Recommendations*, FATF/OECD, Paris, http://www.fatf-gafi.org/media/fatf/documents/recommendations/pdfs/FATF%20Recommendations%202012.pdf..

Ferguson, M. and C. Steverango (2013), *Maximizing the Potential of the Foreign Trade Zone Concept in Canada, McMaster Institute for Transportation and Logistics*, McMaster University, Hamilton, http://mitl.mcmaster.ca/reports/MITL_FTZ_Report.pdf.

Foreign-Trade Zone Resource Center (2017), *Foreign-Trade Zone History*, http://www.foreign-trade-zone.com/history.htm (accessed on 9 December 2017).

Foreign-Trade Zones Board (2016), *77th Annual Report of the Foreign-Trade Zones Board to the Congress of the United States*, Foreign-Trade Zones Board, Springfield, http://enforcement.trade.gov/ftzpage/annualreport/ar-2015.pdf.

Foreign-Trade Zones Resource Center (2017), *Foreign-Trade Zone Benefits*, http://www.foreign-trade-zone.com/benefits.htm (accessed on 9 December 2017).

GAO (1984), *Foreign-Trade Zones Growth Primarily Benefits Users Who Import for Domestic Commerce*, GAO/GGD 84-52, United States General Accounting Office, Gaithersburg, http://www.gao.gov/assets/150/141214.pdf.

GAO (1989), *Foreign-Trade Zones Program Needs Clarified Criteria*, GAO/NSAID-89-85, United States General Accounting Office, Gaithersburg, http://www.gao.gov/assets/150/147348.pdf.

Hainsworth, J. (2017), *Secret foreign trade zone benefits every shipper must know*, The Calgary Region, Canada, http://www.investcalgaryregion.ca/blog/secret-foreign-trade-zone-benefits-shippers-must-know (accessed on 9 December 2017).

Hainsworth, J. (2017), *What is a foreign trade zone and how your business can benefit.*, The Calgary Region, Canada, http://www.investcalgaryregion.ca/blog/ foreign-trade-zone-how-your-business-can-benefit (accessed on 9 December 2017).

Haussman, R., J. Obach and M. Santos (2016), *Special Economic Zones in Panama: Technology Spillovers from a Labor Market Perspective*, Center for International Development Working Paper, Harvard University, https://growthlab.cid.harvard.edu/files/growthlab/files/sez_panama_wp_326.pdf.

Hong Kong Trade Development Council (2017), *HKTDC Forum: Customs & Tariffs - Duty and VAT rules in PRC designated economic areas*, http://forum.hktdc.com/topic.php?id=789&lang=en&page=1 (accessed on 9 December 2017).

ILO (2014), *Trade Union Manual on Export Processing Zones*, International Labour Organization, Geneva, http://www.ilo.org/wcmsp5/groups/public/---ed_dialogue/---actrav/documents/publication/wcms_324632.pdf.

International Trademark Association (2006), *Board Resolution on The Role of Free Trade Zones and Free Ports in the Transshipment and Transit of Counterfeit Goods*, http://www.inta.org/Advocacy/Pages/RoleofFreeTradeZonesandFreePortsintheTransshipmentandTransitofCounterfeitGoods.aspx (accessed on 9 December 2017).

ITA (2016), *Sell Through Panama's Colon Free Trade Zone to the Region – A U.S. Export Opportunity*, The International Trade Administration, U.S. Department of Commerce, https://2016.export.gov/PANAMA/doingbusinessinpanama/exportingtolatinamericathroughpanama/index.asp.

Jafza (2017), *Jebel Ali Freezone*, http://jafza.ae.

Jayanthakumaran, K. (2003), "Benefit-Cost Appraisals of Export Processing Zones: A Survey of the Literature", *Development Policy Review*, Vol. 21/1, pp. 51-65.

Kaufmann, D., A. Kraay and M. Mastruzzi (2010), *The Worldwide Governance Indicators: Methodology and Analytical Issues*, World Bank Policy Research Working Paper No. 5430, World Bank, Washington, DC, http://papers.ssrn.com/sol3/papers.cfm?abstract_id=1682130.

Kennedy, G. (2017), *Setting up as a freelancer in the UAE*, Virtuzone, http://vz.ae/2017/05/24/setting-up-as-a-freelancer-in-the-uae (accessed on 9 December 2017).

Lang Lasalle, J. (2013), *Could Colombia's Free Trade Regime Benefit your Supply Chain?*, http://cscmpaz.org/wp-content/uploads/2015/09/Colombias-Free-Trade-Regime.pdf (accessed on 9 December 2017).

Moore Stephens International (2006), *Doing Business in Panama*, http://worldservicesgroup.com/guides/DBI%20PANAMA%20ENGLISH%209nov06.pdf (accessed on 9 December 2017).

OECD/EUIPO (2016), *Trade in Counterfeit and Pirated Goods: Mapping the Economic Impact*, OECD Publishing, Paris, http://dx.doi.org/10.1787/9789264252653-en.

Pancanada (2017), *Panama as Headquarters for Canadian Multinationals*, Panama-Canada Chamber of Commerce, http://www.pancanada.org/wp-content/uploads/2014/07/Panama-as-Headquarters-for-Canadian-Multinationals-modelo-2-2014.pdf [(accessed on 9 December 2017).

Papadopoulus, N. and S. Malhotra (2007), "Export Processing Zones in Development and International Marketing: An Integrative Review and Research Agenda", *Journal of Macromarketing*, Vol. 27/2, http://dx.doi.org/10.1177/0276146707300070.

Petch, N. (2017), *Nine reasons for entrepreneurs to set up in UAE free zones*, Virtuzone, http://vz.ae/2017/01/26/nine-reasons-entrepreneurs-set-uae-free-trade-zones/ (accessed on 9 December 2017).

PRONTO (2015), *Protectionist nature of certain tax regulations*, Working Paper, Productivity, Non-Tariff Measures and Openness, World Trade Institute, University of Bern, http://pronto.wti.org/media/filer_public/39/58/39581729-7e27-4c1a-8688-b4aa3e05593a/d21v02092015for_wti_wps.pdf.

PRONTO (2017), *Database on Export Processing Zones*, Productivity, Non-Tariff Measures and Openness, World Trade Institute, University of Bern, http://prontonetwork.org/pages/resources.html (accessed on November 2017).

Shadikhodjaev, S. (2011), "International regulation of free zones: An analysis of multilateral customs and trade rules", *World Trade Review*, Vol. 10, pp. 189-216, http://dx.doi.org/10.1017/S1474745611000085.

Torres, R. (2007), "Free Zones and the World Trade Organization Agreement on Subsidies and Countervailing Measures", *Global Trade and Customs Journal*, Vol. 2/5.

U.S. Customs and Border Protection (2017), *User fee - Merchandise Processing Fees*, https://help.cbp.gov/app/answers/detail/a_id/334/~/user-fee---merchandise-processing-fees.

UAE Government (2017), *Starting a business in a free zone*, The Official Portal of the UAE Government, https://government.ae/en/information-and-services/business/starting-a-business-in-a-free-zone (accessed on 9 December 2017).

UN (2017), *Least Developed Countries (LDCs)*, United Nations, Development Policy & Analysis Division, Geneva, http://www.un.org/development/desa/dpad/least-developed-country-category.html. (accessed on 9 December 2017).

UNCTAD (2002), *World Investment Report 2002: Transnational Corporations and Export Competitiveness*, United Nations Conference on Trade and Development, Geneva, http://unctad.org/en/docs/wir2002_en.pdf.

UNCTAD (2013), *World Investment Report 2013_Global Value Chains: Investment and Trade for Development*, United Nations Conference on Trade and Development, Geneva, http://unctad.org/en/PublicationsLibrary/wir2013_en.pdf.

UNCTAD (2015), *Enhancing the Contribution of Export Processing Zones to the Sustainable Development Goals: An analysis of 100 EPZs and a Framework for Sustainable Economic Zones*, United Nations Conference on Trade and Development, Geneva, http://unctad.org/en/PublicationsLibrary/wir2013_en.pdf.

United Nations Statistics Division (2017), *UN Comtrade*, United Nations Statistics Division, New York.

United States Department of Treasury (2002), *Treasury announcing the signing of multilateral recommendations for combatting the black market peso exchange system*, https://www.treasury.gov/press-center/press-releases/Pages/po2001.aspx (accessed on 9 December 2017).

USITC (1984), *The Implications of Foreign Trade Zones for U.S. Industries and for Competitive Conditions Between U.S. and Foreign Firms*, USITC publication 1496, United States International Trade Commission, Washington, http://www.usitc.gov/publications/332/pub1496.pdf.

USITC (1988), *The Implications of Foreign Trade Zones for U.S. Industries and for Competitive Conditions Between U.S. and Foreign Firms*, USITC publication 2059, United States International Trade Commission, Washington, http://www.usitc.gov/publications/332/pub1496.pdf.

WCO (1999), *International Convention on the Simplification and Harmonization of Customs Procedures (as amended)*, World Customs Organization, Brussels,, http://www.wcoomd.org/-/media/wco/public/global/pdf/topics/facilitation/instruments-and-tools/conventions/kyoto-convention/.

Wikipedia Contributors (2017), *Foreign-trade zones of the United States*, Wikipedia, The Free Encyclopedia, https://en.wikipedia.org/wiki/Foreign-trade_zones_of_the_United_States (accessed on 9 December 2017).

World Bank (2017), *Special Economic Zones : An Operational Review of Their Impacts*, World Bank, Washington, DC, https://openknowledge.worldbank.org/handle/10986/29054.

World Bank (2017), *World Bank National Accounts Data*, World Bank, Washington, DC, https://data.worldbank.org/indicator/NY.GDP.PCAP.CD (accessed on November 2017).

World Economic Forum (2016), *The Global Competitiveness Report 2014-2015*, World Economic

Forum, Geneva, http://reports.weforum.org/global-competitiveness-report-2014-2015.

WTO (2008), *Report of the Working Party on the Accession of Ukraine to the World Trade Organization*, WT/ACC/UKR/152, World Trade Organization, Geneva, http://docsonline.wto.org/Dol2FE/Pages/FormerScriptedSearch/directdoc.aspx?DDFDocuments/t/wt/acc/ukr152.doc.

WTO (2017), *Agreement on Subsidies and Countervailing Measures ("SCM Agreement")*, World Trade Organization, Geneva, http://www.wto.org/english/tratop_e/scm_e/subs_e.htm (accessed on 9 December 2017).

Yücer, A., J. Siroën and E. Archanskaia (2014), *World FTZ Database*, http://ftz.dauphine.fr (accessed on November 2017).

4. The institutional framework to combat illicit trade activities in FTZs

While FTZs have existed for some time, in more recent decades their operation has been subject to international agreements, notably those of the World Trade Organization (WTO) and the World Customs Organization (WCO). The possibility of the misuse of FTZs for the purposes of illicit trade, for which the previous chapter provides some solid evidence, has also prompted a number of actors to foster multilateral actions to strengthen the regulation of zone activities. Most have focused on developing recommendations to more effectively combat corruption and money laundering.

The purpose of this chapter is to present some of the institutional frameworks that exist within a range of relevant organisations.

4.1. World Trade Organization

WTO agreements address issues on a countrywide basis and, as such, they do not specifically address free trade zones. The benefits and features of zones are, however, by their very nature discriminatory, and they raise issues with respect to a number of WTO instruments. Interest in monitoring zone operations is reflected in the 1994 Ministerial Decision on Notification Procedures that was included as an annex to the Final Act Embodying the Results of the Uruguay Round of Multilateral Trade Negotiations (Shadikhodjaev, 2011[44]).[1] Under the decision, members agreed to notify each other on the introduction or modification of a number of measures, including, with explicit mention made of free-trade zones. In addition to general notification, a number of WTO agreements have separate notification requirements which may have implications for zones, particularly when certain benefits that target the zones are introduced or maintained.

Zones have also been the object of some scrutiny during the course of accession proceedings in the WTO. In the case of Ukraine, questions were raised about the duty-free treatment of articles exported from zones to Ukraine's customs territory, when significant value had been added in the zone (Creskoff and Walkenhorst, 2009[45]; WTO, 2008[46]). Moreover, zones figure in the accession commitment protocols made by certain new WTO members. The protocols do not use uniform language and underscore the intention of countries to abide by WTO rules in matters pertaining to zones, as follows (Shadikhodjaev, 2011[44]):

> *"The representative of [X] stated that [X] would administer free zones or special economic areas established in its territory in compliance with WTO provisions, including those addressing subsidies, TRIMs and TRIPS, and that goods produced within the zones under tax and tariff provisions that exempt imports and imported inputs from tariffs and certain taxes would be subject to normal customs formalities when entering the rest of [X], including the application of tariffs and any taxes and charges."*

It should be noted that the TRIPS Agreement does not make specific reference to FTZs, which means that it does not exclude its application in FTZs. This means that WTO members are obliged to apply the IPR border measures and criminal measures laid down in the TRIPS Agreement also in FTZs. This interpretation is consistent with the treatment of FTZs in other WTO agreements that address FTZs. It is important to highlight though that due to the special customs treatment of the zones, some countries, mainly the developing countries have misinterpreted the customs free zone regime as being outside the customs jurisdiction for non-tariff matters and they evade the application of the TRIPS Agreement.

In addition, the TRIPS agreement leaves it to its members to determine what sanctions, if any, are to be applied to counterfeit goods transiting their territories. National legal frameworks can, for example, provide for the seizure of counterfeits in transit or prior to commercial declaration, or not. With respect to counterfeit and pirated goods imported into or located within WTO Member States, they "shall provide for criminal procedures and penalties to be applied at least in cases of wilful trademark counterfeiting or copyright piracy on a commercial scale. Remedies available shall include imprisonment and/or monetary fines sufficient to provide a deterrent, consistently with the level of penalties applied for crimes of a corresponding gravity."

4.1.1. Agreement on Subsidies and Countervailing Measures

The WTO Agreement on Subsidies and Countervailing Measures (ASCM) provides a framework governing the treatment of subsidies bestowed by governments. The agreement defines these measures as financial contributions by a government, or private institution acting on its behalf, that provide a benefit to the recipient. These financial contributions may take the form of, i) direct transfers of funds, ii) forgone revenue, iii) provision of goods or services or iv) certain types of price or income supports. Two items which are excluded from the definition are i) support for general infrastructure and ii) the exemption of an exported product from duties or taxes borne by the like product when destined for domestic consumption, or remission of such duties or taxes. WTO jurisprudence has also clarified that the existence of a benefit centres on the question of whether the financial contribution places the recipient in a more advantageous position than would have been the case but for the financial contribution using the marketplace as the basis for comparison. In addition the defined subsidies are covered by WTO regulations only to the extent that they are specific; this essentially occurs when their provision is limited by law or in fact to certain enterprises, industries or regions. The agreement also adds that subsidies which are classified prohibited are presumed to be specific.

The agreement goes on to classify the specific subsidies into different categories according to how trade distortive they are, i) prohibited (those which are contingent on export performance, or on the use of domestic goods over imports), ii) actionable (meaning that they are subject to remedies if they are shown to be having adverse effects) or iii) non-actionable (however the provisions that contemplated this category expired as of the end of 2000). Examples of specific subsidies that have been provided in zones include (Torres, 2007[47]):

- exemption from import duties and charges
- total or partial exemption from direct taxes and social welfare charges
- exemptions from indirect taxes (e.g. sales taxes) and value-added taxes
- provision of goods or services to zone users at below market price.

While benefits to zone users may also include measures such as less onerous labour regulations and/or access to trade facilitating measures, these types of measures are not deemed to constitute financial contributions.

The issue of whether a particular incentive being provided in a zone may be prohibited or actionable under the SCM agreement is a very complex one as it depends not only on the kind of incentive being provided but also on the conditions for establishment and operation in a zone. For example, requirements that zone users export a part of their production, or that they use a prescribed level of domestically produced inputs in their operations (Torres, 2007[47]) will most likely turn many of fiscal incentives provided in the zone into prohibited subsidies. This may also be the case when the government imposes limitations on the extent to which goods in zones may be exported to the domestic market of the host countries as their effect is equivalent to an export requirement. In other cases even if there are no requirements to export, use domestically produced inputs or limitations on sales to the national customs territory the incentives provided in the zones may still qualify as actionable subsidies and are open to challenge by a member under the WTO's dispute settlement mechanism if they cause the kinds of adverse effects contemplated in the agreement. It is also worth noting that regardless of their classification as prohibited or actionable, any specific subsidy may also be subject to countervailing measures by a member receiving the subsidized imports, if it is able to show in the context of a domestic proceeding that these are causing injury to its industry.

In assessing conformity of the different incentives provided in zones one of the more significant items concerns the treatment of production equipment used in zones. Torres (2007)[47] argues that the ASCM provides duty and tax exemptions and remission only for goods used or consumed in a production process. Creskoff and Walkenhorst (2009)[45] suggest that the matter is not so clear, while Shadikhodjaev (2011)[44] accepts the Torres (2007)[47] assessment. With respect to current practice, United States customs allows zone users to defer duty on production equipment that is intended for use in a zone, until such time as the equipment goes into use; at that point any duties and taxes would be applied (CBP, 2011[48]). A review of promotional material for a number of other zones, including those in China (Hong Kong Trade Development Council, 2017[49]), Colombia (Lang Lasalle, 2013[50]), Malaysia (Chai and Im, 2009[51]) and Panama (Moore Stephens International, 2006[52]) indicate that such equipment has been accorded duty and tax-free status during the past decade (i.e. the current situation has not been confirmed).

Another grey area concerns support for infrastructure development (Creskoff and Walkenhorst, 2009[45]). While provision of general infrastructure falls outside the scope of the ASCM, certain types of support, to a designated region, may be deemed specific and therefore actionable. Moreover, a requirement that a zone user manage exports and sales to the domestic market to meet government criteria could transform infrastructure support, as well as other support measures, into a prohibited subsidy. Other questions mentioned by (Creskoff and Walkenhorst, 2009[45]) concern issues relating to the productive organization of countries, particularly with respect to subsidies that are provided to zone businesses that export most of their production without a formal government requirement to do so. In this regard, the ASCM indicates that when the facts demonstrate that there is a relation of conditionality or contingency between the granting of the subsidy and the expectation of exports or export income, it can be considered as prohibited, even if there is no formal export requirement. However this determination of *de facto* contingency will require an examination of all relevant facts and it has been clarified by WTO jurisprudence that the export orientation of the producer is pertinent in this examination but not decisive.

Table 4.1. Countries with extensions for phasing out export subsidies, or reservation of rights to maintain such subsidies

Country	Notified programme(programmes mentioning zones bolded)	WTO action
Antigua and Barbuda	Free trade/processing zones. Fiscal Incentives Act	Granted
Barbados	Fiscal incentive programme. Export allowance. Research & development allowance. International business incentives. Societies with restricted liability. Exports re-discount facility. Export credit insurance scheme. Export finance guarantee scheme. Export grant & incentive scheme.	Granted
Belize	Export Processing Zone Act. Commercial Free Zone Act. Fiscal incentives programme. Conditional duty exemption facility.	Granted
Bolivia	Free zone. Temporary regime for inward processing.	Reservation of rights
Costa Rica	Duty free zone regime. Inward processing regime. Fiscal incentives programme.	Granted
Dominica	Fiscal incentives programme.	Granted
Dominican Republic	Law to Promote the Establishment of Free Trade Zones.	Granted
El Salvador	Export Processing Zones & Marketing Act.	Granted
Fiji	Export processing factories/zones scheme. Short-term export profit deduction.	Granted
Grenada	Fiscal Incentives Act. Qualified Enterprise Act. Statutory rules and orders.	Granted
Guatemala	Free zones. Industrial and free zones (ZOLIC). Special customs regimes.	Granted
Honduras	Free trade zone of Puerto Cortes. Export processing zones. Temporary import regime.	Reservation of rights
Jamaica	Export Free Zone Act. Export Industry Encouragement Act. Foreign Sales Corporation Act. Industrial Incentives Act.	Granted
Jordan	Income Tax Law Act of 1985, amended.	Granted
Kenya	Export processing zones. Export promotion programme. Customs and excise regulation.	Reservation of rights
Mauritius	Freeport scheme. Export enterprise scheme. Export promotion.	Granted
Panama	Export processing zones. Official industry register.	Granted
Papua New Guinea	Income Tax Act.	Granted
Sri Lanka	Income tax concessions. Tax holidays & profits generated. Concessionary tax on dividends. Indirect tax concessions-internal tax exemptions. Export development investment support scheme. Import duty exemption. Exemption from exchange control.	Reservation of rights
St. Kitts & Nevis	Fiscal Incentives Act.	Granted
St. Lucia	Free Zone Act. Fiscal Incentives Act. Micro & Small Business Enterprise Act.	Granted
St. Vincent and the Grenadines	Fiscal Incentives Act.	Granted
Uruguay	Automotive industry export promotion regime.	Granted

Source: (Creskoff and Walkenhorst, 2009[45]).

With respect to the special and differential treatment provided to developing countries, under the provisions of the ASCM, WTO members designated by the United Nations as least-developed countries (UN, 2017[53]), and developing members with less than USD 1 000 per capita GNP are exempted from the export subsidy prohibition. Other developing countries were given until the end of 2002 to phase out their export subsidies; transition economies, on the other hand were given until the end of 2001 (WTO, 2017[54]). In 2001 a number of small economies made the case that some export related fiscal incentives were still important to achieve their industrialization objectives and were permitted to extend the deadline for ending certain specific programmes through the end of 2013, with phase-out required by 31 December 2015 (Creskoff and Walkenhorst, 2009[45]; Torres, 2007[47]).[2] As shown in Table 4.1, many of the requests for extensions explicitly mentioned zones.

4.1.2. Other WTO provisions

In addition to the ASCM, provisions of other WTO agreements may also have implications for zones, including (Creskoff and Walkenhorst, 2009[45]):

- Most favoured nation (MFN) treatment (GATT Article I): The MFN principle requires governments to refrain from taking measures that discriminate between goods or services on the basis of the country of origin.

National treatment (GATT Article III): The national treatment principle calls for governments to refrain from taking measures that favour domestic goods.

- Limitation of fees and formalities connected with importation and exportation to the approximate cost of the services rendered [GATT Article VIII (1)]: The limitation calls for governments to refrain from imposing fees on the processing of imports and exports that exceed the cost of services rendered.
- Transparency requirements (GATT Article X): The requirement calls for governments to refrain from imposing generally applicable trade requirements that have not been published.
- Elimination of quantitative restrictions (GATT Article XI); the provision on quantitative restrictions calls on governments not to prohibit or restrict certain imports and exports that are not justified by applicable WTO exceptions.

In addition, under the General Agreement on Trade in Services (GATS), WTO members must afford treatment to member countries that is no less favourable than the one afforded to like services and service suppliers of any other country (GATS Article II).[3] The national treatment obligation under Article XVII of the GATS obliges WTO members to accord to the services and service suppliers of any other Member treatment no less favourable than is accorded to like domestic services and service suppliers, in those service sectors where specific comments have been made.[4] Under the Agreement on Trade-Related Investment Measures (TRIMS), any zone with a local content requirement, a trade balancing requirement or a foreign exchange requirement would be in violation of GATT Article III or Article XI

4.2. World Customs Organization

The World Customs Organization's International Convention on the Simplification and Harmonization of Customs Procedures (as amended) or the Revised Kyoto Convention[5] provides a blueprint for harmonised customs procedures. The Convention has three substantial parts, i) a body, ii) a general annex and iii) specific annexes (Shadikhodjaev, 2011[44]). Each party is bound by the general annex, while the specific annexes are optional. A party that signs on to a specific annex is bound to abide by all its provisions, but is free to make reservations to any of the recommended practices.

Chapter 2 of Specific Annex D concerns free zones, which are defined here as a "part of the territory of a Contracting Party where any goods introduced are generally regarded, insofar as import duties and taxes are concerned, as being outside the Customs territory"

(WCO, 1999[55]). The word "generally" in the definition leaves open the possibility that some items, such as machinery and equipment located permanently in the zone, may not be considered to be outside the customs territory (Shadikhodjaev, 2011[44]). Goods in zones are normally subject to flexible customs control, usually limited to general checks of goods. Where relevant, they are subject to the provisions of the General Annex, which include, among other things, the rules on clearance and other customs formalities, duties and taxes, and customs control. The chapter sets out 17 standards and four recommended practices, grouped into 10 topic areas. The following is based on the WCO text (WCO, 1999[55]) and the Shadikhodjaev (2011)[44] assessment.

4.2.1. Establishment and controls

There are three standards: i) national legislation must provide for the establishment of zones, admissible goods and permitted operations; ii) customs must articulate the arrangement for customs controls in zones, as well as requirements on the layout and construction of zones; and iii) customs must have the right to carry out checks at any time on goods stored in zones.

4.2.2. Admission of goods

There are three standards. In summary, admission of goods into a zone must include domestic as well as foreign goods, and goods entitled to duty/tax exemptions or repayment when exported must qualify for this upon entry in zones. Two practices are recommended: i) allowing all goods to enter except those raising issues with respect to a) public morality, public security and health, or veterinary or phytosanitary concerns, or b) protection of intellectual property rights (i.e., trademarks, copyrights and patents); and ii) waiving the requirement of a goods declaration, if the information is already available on the documents accompanying the goods.

4.2.3. Security

There is one recommended practice. Customs authorities usually require zone users to provide security to cover customs procedures. The Convention recommends that no such security be required for goods entering zones.

4.2.4. Authorised operations

There are two standards: i) operations for the preservation and handling of goods in zones, including handling to improve their packaging or marketable quality or to prepare them for shipment, must be allowed; and ii) rules on processing or manufacturing operations must be specified.

4.2.5. Goods consumed within the free zone

There is one standard: national legislation must indicate the cases in which goods consumed in zones may be admitted free of duties and taxes and must lay out the requirements which must be met. According to complementary guidelines, the range of goods that can be granted free admission in this regard is broad, and could include, among other things, equipment to be used in the zone, goods consumed by workers in the zone and construction materials.

4.2.6. Duration of stay

There is one standard: duration of the stay of goods in zones must be limited only in exceptional circumstances. The guidelines indicate that these circumstances might include time limits on production or processing, taking into account the nature of the goods and health and safety considerations.

4.2.7. Transfer of ownership

There is one standard: the transfer of ownership of goods in zones must be allowed. The guidelines suggest that retail sales in zones may, however, be prohibited as they can be treated as clearance sales for home use.

4.2.8. Removal of goods

There are two standards: i) the movement of goods to another zone must be permitted or conducted under an applicable customs procedure; and ii) the only declaration required for goods being removed from a zone must be the declaration normally required for the customs procedure to which the goods are assigned. One practice is recommended: when goods are exported from a zone, customs should not require more information than is already available on the documents accompanying the goods.

4.2.9. Assessment of duties and taxes

There are two standards: i) national legislation must specify the point in time to determine the value and quantity of goods being moved into the host country's home economy, and the duties and taxes applicable to such goods; and ii) legislation must specify the rules for determining the duties and taxes due on goods which have been processed or manufactured in zones. The guidelines point out that tax and duty rates may change during the period of time that goods are in zones, and that providing rules gives zone enterprises greater certainty as to how this matter is to be addressed.

4.2.10. Closure of zones

There is one standard: in the event a zone is closed, the parties concerned must be given sufficient notice and time to transport their goods to another zone or place them under a customs procedure.

As of August 2017, of the 112 of the WCO 182 members that had signed the Kyoto Convention, only 24 members had adopted the free zones annex; five of these parties did so with reservations on the recommended practices (Table 4.2). Only three OECD countries were among the parties which signed on to the annex: Korea, Switzerland and the United States.

Table 4.2. Countries having accepted Chapter 2 (on free zones) of Annex D of the Revised Kyoto Convention, as of August 2017

Country	Reservations to recommended practices
Algeria	None
Azerbaijan	None
Benin	None
Burkina Faso	None
China	Practices 6 (grounds for barring admission of goods), 9 and 18 (documentation procedures), and 10 (posting of security)
Cameroon	None
Côte d'Ivoire	None
Egypt	None
Gabon	None
Kazakhstan	None
Korea	Practice 9 (documentation procedures)
Lao People's Democratic Republic	None
Madagascar	None
Malawi	None
Mauritius	Practice 9 (documentation procedures)
Niger	None
Papua New Guinea	None
Senegal	None
Switzerland	None
Togo	None
Tunisia	None
Uganda	Practice 9 (documentation procedures)
Ukraine	None
United States	Practices 9 and 18 (both concern documentation procedures)
Zimbabwe	None

Source: See WCO (1999)[55].

4.3. Other multilateral bodies

Zones have been subject to a number of other multilateral actions, focusing primarily on ways to strengthen efforts to combat corruption and money laundering. This can include a range of instruments, from guidelines, to benchmarking reports that can exert pressure through publishing an assessment of vulnerabilities.

4.3.1. Other international organisation and multilateral initiatives

Caribbean Financial Action Task Force

The Caribbean Financial Action Task Force developed guidelines specific to free trade zones in 2001. The guidelines, entitled *Money Laundering Prevention Guidelines for CFATF Member Governments, Free Trade Zone Authorities and Merchants*, called for the development and implementation of comprehensive legislative regimes for free trade zones; such laws would, among other things, set forth the responsibilities of governments, zone authorities and businesses. Measures to improve monitoring of cash and related liquid transactions would be required, as would steps to improve information on zone transactions (FATF, 2010[37]; FATF, 2008[56])

Financial Action Task Force

The Financial Action Task Force (FATF)[6] has established general *International Standards on Combating Money Laundering and the Financing of Terrorism & Proliferation*, as well as complementary guidance on best (FATF, 2012[57]; FATF, 2008[56]). Zones are not specifically mentioned in the standards, but they were subject to examination in a 2010 report, in which specific recommendations were made, namely (FATF, 2010[37]):

- Zones should be examined in light of FATF general recommendations.
- Awareness-raising efforts should be made with the private sector and relevant competent authorities.
- Co-operation needs to be improved between authorities at the national and international levels, as well as with the private sector.
- Greater attention should be paid to increasing transparency and developing effective regulations and controls for zones.

The report also provides an extensive list of red flag indicators to help identify instances of illicit zone activity.

Black Market Peso Exchange System Multilateral Experts Working Group

The Black Market Peso Exchange System Multilateral Experts Working Group, in which government officials from the United States, Panama, Venezuela, Colombia and Aruba participated, along with free trade zone operators and merchants operating in zones, issued a statement in 2002, in which recommendations to combat an extensive money laundering system in the Western Hemisphere were made (United States Department of Treasury, 2002[58]). The short-term recommendations called for i) conducting public outreach programs on the matters with manufacturers, free trade zone operators and merchants, as well as with other persons engaged in international commerce; ii) more adequate screening, registering, and regulating of merchants engaged in international trade; iii) requiring money changers and exchange offices to report to their supervisory agencies information on suspicious or unusual transactions; and improving communication, coordination, and cooperation among law enforcement, regulatory, and supervisory agencies.

Long-term recommendations included improving the collection, quality, and international exchange of trade data, conducting economic, social, political, and/or legal studies of the problem of trade-based money laundering, and encouraging the development and implementation of an electronic customs filing and reporting system that could be used to track the flow of goods being imported, exported, or transshipped from, to, or through each jurisdiction's customs territory and free trade zones.

4.3.2. Business and private sector initiatives

International Chamber of Commerce

The International Chamber of Commerce, through its Business Action to Stop Counterfeiting and Piracy (BASCAP), published an assessment of the vulnerabilities of zones to criminal activity in 2013 (BASCAP, 2013[59]). The report includes a number of examples of how zones have been used to facilitate illicit trade in counterfeit and pirated products, as well as a series of recommendations to address the matter. These include actions that could be taken by the World Customs Organization (7 actions proposed), the World Trade Organization (2 actions), national governments (5 actions), and zone operators (5 actions).

4.3.3. *International Trademark Association*

The International Trademark Association in 2006 adopted a resolution calling on governments to take actions to halt the trans-shipment and transit of counterfeit goods through zones by (International Trademark Association, 2006[60]):

- prohibiting the admission to, processing in, and export from the free trade zones of counterfeit goods, irrespective of country of origin of such goods, country from which such goods arrived, or country of destination of such goods
- empowering customs authorities to exercise their jurisdiction before the entry and after the exit of goods into a free trade zone, and to inspect goods in a free trade zone or a free port to ensure that no offence as to trafficking in counterfeit goods is being committed
- ensuring close cooperation between national customs authorities and the special authorities of their free trade zones or free ports in order to provide for the efficient enforcement of anti-counterfeiting criminal and civil laws to investigate the offences of trafficking in counterfeit goods
- ensuring the applicability and enforcement of anti-counterfeiting criminal and civil laws to monitor counterfeit goods trafficking activities in the free trade zones and free ports that currently allow free movement of goods of any nature without regard to origin, quality, purpose, and destination of goods; and without any or with only minimal customs treatment of such goods in transit or transhipment.
-

Notes

[1] See www.wto.org/english/docs_e/legal_e/33-dnotf_e.htm#fnt-1.

[2] See also www.wto.org/english/news_e/news12_e/scm_23oct12_e.htm.

[3] GATS Article II allows WTO members to accord advantages to adjacent countries in order to facilitate exchanges limited to contiguous frontier zones of services that are both locally produced and consumed.

[4] A Member wishing to maintain any limitations on national treatment, i.e. any measures which result in less-favourable treatment of foreign services or service suppliers, must indicate so in its schedule of specific commitments.

[5] The convention is commonly referred to as the Revised Kyoto Convention.

[6] The FATF currently comprises 35 member economies and 2 regional organisations, representing most major financial centres in all parts of the globe. See: http://www.fatf-gafi.org

References

BASCAP (2013), *Controlling the Zone: Balancing facilitation and control to combat illicit trade in the world's Free Trade Zones*, Business Action to Stop Counterfeiting and Piracy, International Chamber of Commerce, Paris, https://cdn.iccwbo.org/content/uploads/sites/3/2016/11/Combating-illicit-trade-in-FTZs-1.pdf.

Carribbean Financial Action Task Force (2000), *Money Laundering Prevention Guidelines for CFATF Member Governments, Free Trade Zone Authorities, and Merchants*, http://www.cfatf-gafic.org/index.php/documents/archives/22-free-trade-zone-recommendations-english/file (accessed on 9 December 2017).

CBP (2011), *Foreign-Trade Zones Manual*, US Customs and Border Protection, Department of Homeland Security, http://www.cbp.gov/sites/default/files/documents/FTZmanual2011.pdf.

CEPII (2017), *GRAVITY Database*, http://www.cepii.fr/CEPII/en/bdd_modele/presentation.asp?id=14 (accessed on November 2017).

Chai, Y. and O. Im (2009), *The Development of Free Industrial Zones – The Malaysian Experience*, http://share.nanjing-school.com/dpgeography/files/2012/10/info.worldbank.org-s9hsat.pdf (accessed on 9 December 2017).

Creskoff, S. and P. Walkenhorst (2009), *Implications of WTO Disciplines for Special Economic Zones in Developing Countries,*, Policy Research Working Paper 4892, World Bank, Washington, DC, http://www.researchgate.net/profile/Peter_Walkenhorst/publication/228239934_Implications_of_WTO_Disciplines_for_Special_Economic_Zones_in_Developing_Countries/links/54fd4ee90cf270426d11ca5d/Implications-of-WTO-Disciplines-for-Special-Economic-Zones-in-Developing.

FATF (2008), *Best Practices Paper: Best Practices on Trade Based Money Laundering*, FATF/OECD, Paris, http://www.fatf-gafi.org/media/fatf/documents/recommendations/BPP%20Trade%20Based%20Money%20Laundering%202012%20COVER.pdf.

FATF (2012), *International Standards on Combating Money Laundering and the Financing of Terrorism & Proliferation: The FATF Recommendations*, FATF/OECD, Paris, http://www.fatf-gafi.org/media/fatf/documents/recommendations/pdfs/FATF%20Recommendations%202012.pdf..

Foreign-Trade Zone Resource Center (2017), *Foreign-Trade Zone History*, http://www.foreign-trade-zone.com/history.htm (accessed on 9 December 2017).

Hong Kong Trade Development Council (2017), *HKTDC Forum: Customs & Tariffs - Duty and VAT rules in PRC designated economic areas*, http://forum.hktdc.com/topic.php?id=789&lang=en&page=1 (accessed on 9 December 2017).

International Trademark Association (2006), *Board Resolution on The Role of Free Trade Zones and Free Ports in the Transshipment and Transit of Counterfeit Goods*, http://www.inta.org/Advocacy/Pages/RoleofFreeTradeZonesandFreePortsintheTransshipmentandTransitofCounterfeitGoods.aspx (accessed on 9 December 2017).

Kennedy, G. (2017), *Setting up as a freelancer in the UAE*, Virtuzone, http://vz.ae/2017/05/24/setting-up-as-a-freelancer-in-the-uae (accessed on 9 December 2017).

Lang Lasalle, J. (2013), *Could Colombia's Free Trade Regime Benefit your Supply Chain?*, http://cscmpaz.org/wp-content/uploads/2015/09/Colombias-Free-Trade-Regime.pdf (accessed on 9 December 2017).

Moore Stephens International (2006), *Doing Business in Panama*, http://worldservicesgroup.com/guides/DBI%20PANAMA%20ENGLISH%209nov06.pdf (accessed on 9 December 2017).

Shadikhodjaev, S. (2011), "International regulation of free zones: An analysis of multilateral customs and trade rules", *World Trade Review*, Vol. 10, pp. 189-216, http://dx.doi.org/10.1017/S1474745611000085.

Torres, R. (2007), "Free Zones and the World Trade Organization Agreement on Subsidies and Countervailing Measures", *Global Trade and Customs Journal*, Vol. 2/5.

UN (2017), *Least Developed Countries (LDCs)*, United Nations, Development Policy & Analysis Division, Geneva, http://www.un.org/development/desa/dpad/least-developed-country-category.html. (accessed on 9 December 2017).

United States Department of Treasury (2002), *Treasury announcing the signing of multilateral recommendations for combatting the black market peso exchange system*, https://www.treasury.gov/press-center/press-releases/Pages/po2001.aspx (accessed on 9 December 2017).

United Nations Statistics Division (2017), *UN Comtrade*, United Nations Statistics Division, New York

WCO (1999), *International Convention on the Simplification and Harmonization of Customs Procedures (as amended)*, World Customs Organization, Brussels,, http://www.wcoomd.org/-/media/wco/public/global/pdf/topics/facilitation/instruments-and-tools/conventions/kyoto-convention/.

World Bank (2017), *World Bank National Accounts Data*, World Bank, Washington, DC, https://data.worldbank.org/indicator/NY.GDP.PCAP.CD (accessed on November 2017).

World Economic Forum (2016), *The Global Competitiveness Report 2014-2015*, World Economic Forum, Geneva, http://reports.weforum.org/global-competitiveness-report-2014-2015.

WTO (2008), *Report of the Working Party on the Accession of Ukraine to the World Trade Organization*, WT/ACC/UKR/152, World Trade Organization, Geneva, http://docsonline.wto.org/Dol2FE/Pages/FormerScriptedSearch/directdoc.aspx?DDFDocuments/t/wt/acc/ukr152.doc.

WTO (2017), *Agreement on Subsidies and Countervailing Measures ("SCM Agreement")*, World Trade Organization, Geneva, http://www.wto.org/english/tratop_e/scm_e/subs_e.htm (accessed on 9 December 2017).

5. Conclusion

This report has quantitatively and qualitatively examined the economic role played by Free Trade Zones, especially in the context of trade in counterfeit and pirated goods. It has done so by analysing the economic rationales for Free Trade Zones from the perspectives of both host countries and industry, and it has conducted an econometric analysis of the role that the FTZs play in spurring trade in counterfeit and pirated goods.

Businesses that operate in zones reap numerous benefits, including savings in taxes and customs duties and being subjected to more flexible labour and immigration rules than those applicable in the customs territories of host countries. Zones also offer lighter regulation and oversight of corporate activities, fewer restrictions on corporate activities, and opportunities to improve distribution of goods to diverse markets.

From the host country perspective, FTZs can and have been used as a tool to promote economic growth, both in developed and developing economies. The potential benefits include attracting foreign investment (particularly in high-tech industries), creating additional jobs and enhancing export performance. In the long term, FTZs are seen as an engine to promote regional development and overall economic modernisation through the improvement of infrastructure, the strengthening of support services and the transfer of technology and knowledge.

However, several arguments have been raised to point to certain disadvantages that FTZs bring to host economies. These include forgone tax revenues due to favourable taxation schemes. FTZs are also often seen as overly permissive, allowing companies operating within them to get away with poor workplace health and safety conditions and to engage in illicit operations due to lax controls and oversight on the part of host countries.

Lightly regulated zones can be particularly attractive to parties engaged in illegal and criminal activities. From the third country, perspective many Free Trade Zones frequently feature among the list of transit points in illicit trade, including trade in counterfeit and pirated goods.

The quantitative analysis presented in this report confirms that FTZs do indeed correlate with higher volumes of trade in counterfeit and pirated goods. These results are statistically robust, taking into account as they do a range of additional factors that could affect the volumes of trade in fakes, including the general level of economic development in the host country, the quality of intellectual property protection, the efficiency of customs and the overall volume of trade.

After controlling for all these variables, the study found that the existence, number and size of FTZs increase the value of counterfeit and pirated products exported by a given economy. The findings indicate that one additional FTZs within an economy significantly increases counterfeiting by 5.9% on average. In other words, keeping all other factors constant, the establishment of a new Free Trade Zone in a given economy is likely to result in higher volumes of trade in fakes departing from this economy. Similarly robust results were found for the links between the value of fake goods exported from that economy and the number of firms operating in Zones and the value of exports from these zones.

The results presented here are robust and statistically significant. They constitute a clear indication that FTZs are a particularly useful tool for counterfeiters, who tend to exploit them regularly in their operations.

These results confirm the anecdotal evidence pointing to the misuse of FTZs to conduct illicit trade, and they should be a prompt for future actions. These steps could include the development of clear guidelines for countries to increase transparency and promote clean and fair trade in FTZs. Developing such soft law will require the involvement of industry members and the key stakeholders in the trade chain.

In addition, more in-depth analysis in three areas will be crucial for developing and deepening enforcement and governance frameworks in order to combat the misuse of FTZs in illicit trade. More quantitative research is also needed to improve the precision of assessments of the role of FTZs in comparison with other economies in trade in counterfeit and pirated goods. It would also be necessary to develop a fuller quantitative picture of counterfeit trade at the national level, and to determine why counterfeit profiles look different for economies that otherwise seem similar. For example, such a study could look at the quantitative relationship between the intensities of counterfeiting and free trade indices, the quality of governance and public sector integrity of.

In the light of the challenges highlighted by the evidence produced for this report, a number of international initiatives have been adopted to address some of the issues created by Free Trade Zones. Further work might be required to close some of the remaining gaps and see how to step up policy action in the future, to ensure that countries can retain the benefits of Free Trade Zones for world trade and economic growth, while applying strong deterrents to criminal activities and reducing the value proposition of FTZs for criminal networks.

Annex A. Additional tables

Table A.1. Estimated value of counterfeit and pirated world imports by provenance economies, 2011-2013

Value in USD million

Economy	2011	2012	2013	Economy	2011	2012	2013
Afghanistan	3.8	5.8	8.5	Côte d'Ivoire	46.8	76.3	67.5
Albania	17.6	25.0	26.3	Croatia	93.9	142.0	131.0
Algeria	182.0	0.0	233.0	Cyprus*	69.2	81.5	82.5
Andorra	0.0	0.0	0.0	Czech Republic	1170.0	1790.0	1620.0
Antigua and Barbuda	0.0	0.0	0.0	Denmark	779.0	1170.0	1070.0
Argentina	2140.0	2700.0	2190.0	Dominican Republic	425.0	600.0	657.0
Armenia	9.5	16.4	16.5	Ecuador	70.2	134.0	113.0
Aruba	0.0	2.3	0.0	Egypt	792.0	1000.0	906.0
Australia	766.0	1280.0	987.0	El Salvador	73.6	107.0	104.0
Austria	1090.0	1640.0	1480.0	Estonia	131.0	206.0	185.0
Azerbaijan	0.0	179.0	140.0	Ethiopia	13.6	26.3	28.9
Bahamas	31.8	0.0	0.0	Fiji	0.0	10.1	7.7
Bahrain	94.2	134.0	159.0	Finland	702.0	1010.0	865.0
Bangladesh	1500.0	0.0	0.0	Former Yugoslav Republic of Macedonia	34.9	51.9	50.9
Barbados	0.0	0.0	4.0	France	3980.0	6020.0	5380.0
Belarus	156.0	315.0	215.0	French Polynesia	0.0	0.0	0.0
Belgium	3190.0	4730.0	4640.0	Gambia	0.0	0.7	0.0
Belize	6.3	0.0	8.1	Georgia	8.5	18.1	18.3
Benin	0.0	0.0	7.3	Germany	12800.0	18900.0	17100.0
Bermuda	0.0	0.0	0.0	Ghana	196.0	318.0	223.0
Bhutan	0.0	0.0	0.0	Greece	1320.0	1610.0	1520.0
Bolivia	31.0	83.3	0.0	Greenland	0.0	0.0	0.0
Bosnia and Herzegovina	93.5	125.0	125.0	Guatemala	168.0	239.0	217.0
Botswana	0.0	86.3	0.0	Guyana	0.0	16.5	0.0
Brazil	867.0	1480.0	1210.0	Honduras	24.2	57.8	0.0
Bulgaria	1000.0	1120.0	1140.0	Hong Kong (China)	44500.0	53300.0	54100.0
Burkina Faso	0.0	0.0	25.1	Hungary	843.0	1200.0	1070.0
Burundi	0.0	0.0	3.0	Iceland	0.0	26.6	0.0
Cabo Verde	1.7	2.8	0.0	India	14800.0	17400.0	18300.0
Cambodia	381.0	533.0	587.0	Indonesia	2850.0	3970.0	3370.0
Cameroon	7.9	22.7	0.0	Iran	450.0	0.0	0.0
Canada	3310.0	5190.0	4440.0	Iraq	196.0	409.0	303.0
Central African Republic	0.0	0.0	0.0	Ireland	1190.0	1620.0	1390.0
Chile	218.0	226.0	182.0	Israel	631.0	894.0	830.0
China (People's Republic of)	152000.0	189000.0	193000.0	Italy	4430.0	6630.0	6090.0

Table A.1. Estimated value of counterfeit and pirated world imports by provenance economies, 2011-2013 (*continued*)

Value in USD million

Economy	2011	2012	2013	Economy	2011	2012	2013
Colombia	236.0	425.0	334.0	Palau	0.0	0.0	0.0
Comoros	0.0	0.0	0.0	Palestinian Authority*	0.0	0.0	0.0
Congo	27.5	33.7	36.1	Panama	1390.0	45.5	35.8
Cook Islands	0.0	0.0	0.0	Papua New Guinea	0.0	0.0	0.0
Costa Rica	0.0	128.0	118.0	Paraguay	28.8	48.8	47.7
Jamaica	3.8	0.0	5.3	Peru	526.0	715.0	566.0
Japan	5570.0	8770.0	6730.0	Philippines	745.0	1590.0	1500.0
Jordan	91.0	134.0	125.0	Poland	1230.0	1890.0	1860.0
Kazakhstan	194.0	401.0	277.0	Portugal	0.0	580.0	544.0
Kiribati	0.0	0.3	0.0	Qatar	285.0	617.0	504.0
Korea	4910.0	7950.0	7180.0	Romania	710.0	991.0	982.0
Kyrgyzstan	0.0	18.5	18.4	Russia	1250.0	2760.0	2250.0
Latvia	277.0	407.0	396.0	Rwanda	0.0	0.0	0.0
Lebanon	193.0	260.0	178.0	Saint Kitts and Nevis	0.7	0.0	0.0
Lesotho	0.0	0.0	0.0	Saint Vincent and the Grenadines	0.0	0.0	0.0
Lithuania	167.0	286.0	281.0	Samoa	0.0	0.0	0.0
Luxembourg	0.0	0.0	91.6	Sao Tome and Principe	0.0	0.0	0.0
Macau (China)	53.4	82.2	0.0	Saudi Arabia	1060.0	2020.0	1570.0
Madagascar	0.0	0.0	0.0	Senegal	85.5	124.0	119.0
Malawi	40.0	0.0	0.0	Serbia	69.0	112.0	124.0
Malaysia	4750.0	6620.0	5770.0	Singapore	6400.0	9330.0	8810.0
Maldives	0.0	1.9	0.0	Slovak Republic	511.0	820.0	767.0
Mali	0.0	27.8	0.0	Slovenia	286.0	410.0	382.0
Malta	37.0	59.7	49.7	Solomon Islands	0.0	0.0	0.0
Mauritania	0.0	0.0	0.0	South Africa	685.0	990.0	794.0
Mauritius	63.6	80.3	72.7	Spain	1880.0	2870.0	2750.0
Mexico	2680.0	4460.0	3970.0	Sri Lanka	179.0	229.0	233.0
Micronesia	0.4	0.0	0.0	Sudan	0.0	38.5	0.0
Moldova	33.9	48.6	48.4	Suriname	4.0	4.7	19.1
Montenegro	3.2	4.6	0.0	Sweden	1190.0	1730.0	1490.0
Montserrat	0.0	0.0	0.0	Switzerland	6950.0	12700.0	13500.0
Morocco	1190.0	1340.0	1270.0	Tanzania	46.1	80.5	59.3
Mozambique	0.0	0.0	28.1	Thailand	2880.0	4180.0	3590.0
Namibia	40.3	0.0	0.0	Togo	5.8	9.2	11.1
Nepal	41.1	47.8	44.8	Tonga	0.0	0.0	0.0
Netherlands	3320.0	5080.0	4800.0	Tunisia	880.0	990.0	913.0
New Caledonia	0.7	5.3	0.0	Turkey	7030.0	10400.0	9120.0
New Zealand	151.0	259.0	228.0	Turks and Caicos Islands	0.0	0.0	0.0
Nicaragua	0.0	54.7	52.6	Uganda	0.0	0.0	0.0
Niger	0.0	8.0	0.0	Ukraine	318.0	635.0	506.0
Nigeria	1260.0	2240.0	1180.0	United Arab Emirates	7850.0	16000.0	16800.0
Norway	507.0	0.0	722.0	United Kingdom	4780.0	6560.0	7060.0
Oman	123.0	246.0	210.0	United States	12700.0	20300.0	18000.0
Pakistan	1880.0	1920.0	1970.0	Uruguay	285.0	406.0	353.0

Vanuatu	0.0	0.0	0.0		Yemen	49.0	0.0	64.4
Venezuela	254.0	483.0	348.0		Zambia	34.5	0.0	0.0
Viet Nam	1640.0	2820.0	3090.0		Zimbabwe	0.0	0.0	0.0

Source: Authors' own calculations based on OECD-EUIPO (2016).

Notes: *For Cyprus:

Note by Turkey: The information in this document with reference to "Cyprus" relates to the southern part of the Island. There is no single authority representing both Turkish and Greek Cypriot people on the Island. Turkey recognises the Turkish Republic of Northern Cyprus (TRNC). Until a lasting and equitable solution is found within the context of the United Nations, Turkey shall preserve its position concerning the "Cyprus issue".

Note by all the European Union member states of the OECD and the European Commission: The Republic of Cyprus is recognised by all members of the United Nations with the exception of Turkey. The information in this document relates to the area under the effective control of the Government of the Republic of Cyprus

Table A.2. Existence, number of FTZs and exports of counterfeit and pirated products, 2011-2013 (alter specification)

	Dependant variable: value of counterfeit and pirated exports (in log) by economy and year			
	(1)	(2)	(3)	(4)
Export value (in log)	0.812***	0.767***	0.778***	0.816***
	(0.085)	(0.089)	(0.089)	(0.082)
GDP per capita (in log)	15.575***	15.610***	15.414***	9.930*
	(4.884)	(5.175)	(5.167)	(5.824)
GDP per capita 2 (in log)	-0.736***	-0.731**	-0.716**	-0.483
	(0.266)	(0.283)	(0.283)	(0.315)
Corruption Index	-1.251***	-0.979**	-1.061**	-1.138***
	(0.412)	(0.465)	(0.475)	(0.421)
Time to exports (in days)	-0.129**	-0.143***	-0.143***	-0.193***
	(0.050)	(0.050)	(0.051)	(0.055)
Dummy for EPZ (World FTZ database)	2.614***			
	(0.648)			
Dummy for EPZ (PRONTO)		1.393*		
		(0.761)		
Dummy for pure EPZ (PRONTO)			1.449*	
			(0.786)	
Dummy for SEZ (PRONTO)			0.583	
			(0.675)	
Dummy for EMPZ (PRONTO)			0.004	
			(0.683)	
Number of EPZs				0.053**
				(0.025)
_cons	-82.503***	-80.910***	-80.653***	-48.852*
	(22.493)	(23.713)	(23.655)	(27.086)
Observations	330	330	330	255
Adjusted R2	0.586***	0.567***	0.566***	0.543***
F statistic	43.630 (df='8;' 109)	38.862 (df='8;' 109)	30.839 (df='10;' 109)	30.354 (df='8;' 84)

Notes: Robust standard errors in parentheses. *p<0.1; **p<0.05; ***p<0.01. Estimates are results of Equation 3.1 for the period 2011-2013. As compared to Table 3.4, the sample of economies excludes China and Hong-Kong.

Table A.3. Size of FTZs and exports of counterfeit and pirated products (alter specification)

	Dependant variable: value of counterfeit and pirated exports (in log) by economy and year			
	(1)	(2)	(3)	(4)
Export value (in log)	0.899***	0.872***	0.889***	0.863***
	(0.083)	(0.098)	(0.102)	(0.106)
GDP per capita (in log)	0.865	14.892**	10.834	3.054
	(8.098)	(7.526)	(8.024)	(8.123)
GDP per capita 2 (in log)	-0.066	-0.740*	-0.536	-0.144
	(0.450)	(0.411)	(0.440)	(0.451)
Corruption Index	-0.957*	-1.235**	-1.111*	-1.709***
	(0.519)	(0.579)	(0.624)	(0.612)
Time to exports (in days)	-0.313***	-0.201***	-0.221***	-0.338***
	(0.080)	(0.062)	(0.060)	(0.068)
Value of exports from EPZ	0.257***			
	(0.088)			
Number of firms operating in EPZ (in log)		0.245		
		(0.149)		
Number of employees in EPZs (in log)			0.177*	
			(0.099)	
Value of investment in EPZs (in log)				0.157***
				(0.056)
_cons	-2.858	-75.405**	-55.726	-14.528
	(36.233)	(34.617)	(36.556)	(37.029)
Observations	177	213	213	174
Adjusted R2	0.588***	0.534***	0.538***	0.585***
F statistic	30.092 (df='8;' 58)	24.598 (df='8;' 70)	23.683 (df='8;' 70)	23.115 (df='8;' 57)

Notes: Robust standard errors in parentheses. *p<0.1; **p<0.05; ***p<0.01. Estimates are results of Equation 4.1 for the period 2011-2013. All EPZ-related variables are extracted from the World FTZ database (see Section 3.1). As compared to Table 3.4, the sample of economies excludes China and Hong-Kong.

OECD PUBLISHING, 2, rue André-Pascal, 75775 PARIS CEDEX 16
(42 2018 01 1 P) ISBN 978-92-64-28954-3 – 2018